CHRISTMAS Wonderland ™

Dear Friends,

Remember the excitement you felt as a child when you rushed to the tree on Christmas morning? Experience that feeling again as you behold this unique book filled with an exclusive selection of gift and home decor ideas. Imagine your home, overflowing with inviting needlecraft decorations that add a warm, friendly glow. Imagine the joy on the faces of your youngsters when they receive magical gifts, handmade by you for hours of playtime fun. Imagine the pride and sense of accomplishment you'll feel at giving carefully crafted presents to those you love — chosen especially for them.

The holiday season is an exhilarating time. A time for brilliant colors, twinkling lights, sparkling ornaments and heartwarming togetherness. But best of all it's a time for giving and remembering. And what better way to show your love than by sharing your talents with others in the form of handcrafted gifts and cheerful decorations. You'll receive compliments and praises for all the effort, and the personal delight of knowing you've given something that will be cherished for years to come.

From exquisite angels to illuminate your table or tree, to whimsical characters that will delight the children, to sentimental designs with a religious theme, you'll find something to suit every holiday need. We searched far and wide to bring you this exceptional offering of charming, unforgettable needlecraft projects, and it was worth it! Now you can add an enchanting richness to your holiday festivities beyond compare with fabulous needlecraft projects guaranteed to be tops on everyone's list. With the wide variety of creations from leading designers featured in these pages, your hardest decision will be where to start. Why not begin now?

Happy holiday stitching,

Jennifer

Favorite Ornaments

PUBLISHER: Donna Robertson   DESIGN DIRECTOR: Fran Rohus   PRODUCTION DIRECTOR: Ange Workman

EDITORIAL
SENIOR EDITORS:
Jennifer A. Simcik, Janet Tipton
EDITORS: Nancy Harris, Kristine Hart-Kirst,
Susan Koellner, Sharon Lothrop
EDITOR / ILLUSTRATOR: Pauline Rosenberger
COPY EDITOR: Marianne Telesca

PHOTOGRAPHY
PHOTOGRAPHER: Mary Craft
PHOTO STYLIST / COORDINATOR: Ruth Whitaker

BOOK DESIGN / PRODUCTION
PRODUCTION MANAGER: Glenda Chamberlain

PRODUCT DESIGN
DESIGN COORDINATOR: Brenda Wendling

BUSINESS
CEO: John Robinson
VICE PRESIDENT / CUSTOMER SERVICE: Karen Pierce
VICE PRESIDENT / MARKETING: Greg Deily
VICE PRESIDENT / M.I.S: John Trotter

Credits: Sincerest thanks to all the designers, manufacturers and other professionals whose dedication has made
this book possible. Special thanks to David Norris of Quebecor Printing Book Group, Kingsport, TN.
Copyright © 1995 The Needlecraft Shop, LLC. All rights reserved. No part of this book may be reproduced in any form or by any means without the written
permission of the publisher, excepting brief quotations in connection with reviews written specifically for inclusion in magazines, newspapers and other publications.
Library of Congress Cataloging-in-Publication Data ISBN: 0-9638031-6-6
Library of Congress Catalog Card Number: 95-69228
First Printing: 1995
Published and Distributed by The Needlecraft Shop, LLC. Printed in the United States of America.

A Joyous Welcome

Hark! the Herald Angels Sing

7

Sweet Memories

Snow is Glistening

Dreaming by the Fire

Joy to the World

Silver and Gold

Quick as a Wink Gifts

Just For You

Favorite Ornaments

Heirloom quality ornaments are a
treasure that returns the happiness
of seasons past again and again.
Whether you wish to commemorate
one of life's great events or show love
and appreciation, you'll find something
to suit everyone in this handsome
collection. Perfect for any number
of uses, let your creative imagination
run wild dreaming up new ways to
utilize these festive designs.

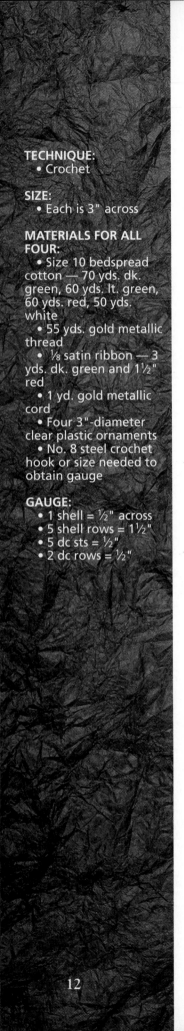

Golden Lace Globes

Designed by Hazel Henry

TECHNIQUE:
• Crochet

SIZE:
• Each is 3" across

MATERIALS FOR ALL FOUR:
• Size 10 bedspread cotton — 70 yds. dk. green, 60 yds. lt. green, 60 yds. red, 50 yds. white
• 55 yds. gold metallic thread
• ⅛ satin ribbon — 3 yds. dk. green and 1½" red
• 1 yd. gold metallic cord
• Four 3"-diameter clear plastic ornaments
• No. 8 steel crochet hook or size needed to obtain gauge

GAUGE:
• 1 shell = ½" across
• 5 shell rows = 1½"
• 5 dc sts = ½"
• 2 dc rows = ½"

ORNAMENT NO. 1
COVER

Rnd 1: With dk. green, ch 8, sl st in first ch to form ring, ch 3, 23 dc in ring, join with sl st in top of ch-3 (24 dc).

NOTES: For **shell,** (2 dc, ch 2, 2 dc) in next st or ch sp.

For **beginning shell (beg shell),** sl st in next st, (sl st, ch 3, dc, ch 3, 2 dc) in next ch sp.

Rnd 2: (Ch 3, dc, ch 2, 2 dc) in first st, ch 4, skip next 2 sts, (shell in next st, ch 4, skip next 2 sts) around, join (8 shells).

Rnd 3: Beg shell, ch 2, sc in next ch-4 sp, ch 2, (shell in ch sp of next shell, ch 2, sc in next ch-4 sp, ch 2) around, join.

Rnd 4: Beg shell, ch 4, (shell in next shell, ch 4) around, join.

Rnd 5: Beg shell, ch 3, sc in next ch-4 sp, ch 3, (shell in next shell, ch 3, sc in next ch-4 sp, ch 3) around, join.

Rnd 6: Beg shell, (ch 3, sc in next ch sp) 2 times, ch 3, *shell in next shell, (ch 3, sc in next ch sp) 2 times, ch 3; repeat from * around, join.

Rnd 7: Beg shell, skip next ch sp, (tr, ch 1) 4 times in next ch sp, tr in same ch sp, skip next ch sp, *shell in next shell, skip next ch sp, (tr, ch 1) 4 times in next ch sp, tr in same ch sp, skip next ch sp; repeat from * around, join.

Rnd 8: Beg shell, (ch 3, sc in next ch-1 sp) 4 times, ch 3, *shell in next shell, (ch 3, sc in next ch-1 sp) 4 times, ch 3; repeat from * around, join.

Rnd 9: Beg shell, *[ch 4, skip next ch sp, (sc in next ch sp, ch 3) 2 times, sc in next ch sp, ch 4, skip next ch sp], shell in next shell; repeat from * 6 more times; repeat between [ ], join.

Rnd 10: Beg shell, *[ch 4, skip next ch sp, sc in next ch sp, ch 3, sc in next ch sp, ch 4, skip next ch sp], shell in next shell; repeat from * 6 more times; repeat between [ ], join.

Rnd 11: Beg shell, ch 4, skip next ch sp, sc in next ch sp, ch 4, skip next ch sp, (shell in next ch sp, ch 4, skip next ch sp, sc in next ch sp, ch 4, skip next ch sp) around, join, fasten off.

Rnd 12: Join metallic thread with sl st in ch sp of any shell, (ch 3, dc, ch 2, 2 dc) in same ch sp, *[dc in each of next 2 dc, 3 dc in each of next 2 ch-4 sps, dc in each of next 2 dc], shell in next shell ch sp; repeat from * 6 more times; repeat between [ ], join.

Rnd 13: Ch 1, sc in each st around with 2 sc in each ch-2 sp, join with sl st in first sc, fasten off (128 sc).

Rnd 14: Join dk. green with sc in 4th st, (ch 5, skip next 3 sts, sc in next st) around to last 3 sts; to **join,** ch 2, skip last 3 sts, dc in first sc (32 ch sps).

Rnds 15-20: Ch 1, sc around joining dc, (ch 5, sc in next ch sp) around; to **join,** ch 2, dc in first st.

Rnd 21: Ch 6, dc in next ch sp, ch 3, (dc in next ch sp, ch 3) around, join with sl st in 3rd ch of ch-6.

Rnd 22: Sl st in each of next 2 chs, ch 1, sc in same ch sp, (ch 5, sc in next ch sp) around; to **join,** ch 2, dc in first sc.

Rnds 23-25: Repeat rnd 15. At end of last rnd, fasten off.

Rnd 26: Join metallic thread with sc in any ch sp, ch 5, (sc in next ch sp, ch 5) around, join with sl st in first sc, fasten off.

FINISHING

1: For hanger, cut 5" strand of metallic thread. Insert one end through hanger at top of plastic ornament; tie ends into a knot.

2: Cut two ¾-yd. lengths of dk. green ribbon. With both pieces held together, weave through ch sps of rnd 17. Insert plastic ornament, pull ribbon ends to gather around ball, tie ends into a bow.

ORNAMENT NO. 2
COVER

Rnd 1: With red, ch 5, sl st in first ch to form ring, ch 1, 8 sc in ring, join with sl st in first sc (8 sc).

NOTES: For **beginning cluster (beg cl),** ch 4, *yo 2 times, insert hook in same st, yo, draw lp through, (yo, draw through 2 lps on hook) 2 times; repeat from *, yo, draw through all 3 lps on hook.

For **cluster (cl),** yo 2 times, insert hook in next st, yo, draw lp through, (yo, draw through 2 lps on hook) 2 times, *yo 2 times, insert hook in same st, yo, draw lp through, (yo, draw through 2 lps on hook) 2 times; repeat from *, yo, draw through all

4 lps on hook.

Rnd 2: Beg cl, ch 3, (cl in next st, ch 3) around, join with sl st in top of first cl (8 cls).

Rnd 3: Beg cl, ch 5, cl in same st, (cl, ch 5, cl) in each cl around, join.

Rnd 4: Sl st in first ch sp, ch 3, 9 dc in same sp, 10 dc in each ch sp around, join with sl st in top of ch-3 (80 dc).

Rnd 5: Ch 3, dc in next st, ch 3, skip next 2 sts, (dc in each of next 2 sts, ch 3, skip next 2 sts) around, join (40 dc, 20 ch sps).

Rnd 6: Sl st in next st, sl st in next ch sp, ch 3, 4 dc in same sp, 5 dc in each ch sp around, join (100 dc).

Rnd 7: Sl st in next 4 sts, (sl st, ch 3, dc) in next sp between 5-dc groups, ch 3; working in sps between 5-dc groups, (2 dc in next

Continued on page 19

TECHNIQUE:
• Plastic Canvas

SIZE:
• Each is about 1¾" long

MATERIALS:
• One sheet of 14-count plastic canvas
• ¹⁄₁₆" metallic ribbon or heavy metallic braid (for amount see Color Key on page 27)
• #5 pearl cotton or six-strand embroidery floss (for amounts see Color Key)

Tiny Additions

Designed by Celia Lange Designs

CUTTING INSTRUCTIONS
NOTE: Graphs on page 27.
A: For Ornaments #1-#7, cut three each according to graphs.

STITCHING INSTRUCTIONS
1: Using pearl cotton or six strands floss in colors and stitches indicated, work A pieces according to graphs. Using colors indicated, Backstitch and Cross Stitch, embroider detail as indicated on #1, #3, #4 and #6 graphs.

2: For each Ornament, with white for #1, red for #2-#4 and with green, Whipstitch matching pieces together, leaving a loop at top for hanger (see photo).❊

Victorian Trinkets

Designed by Jocelyn Sass

CUTTING INSTRUCTIONS

NOTE: Graphs on page 27.

A: For Angel, cut one according to graph.

B: For Hanger, cut one according to graph.

STITCHING INSTRUCTIONS

1: Using colors and stitches indicated, work A and B pieces according to graphs. With gold cord for halo and with matching colors, Overcast unfinished edges.

2: For Angel hanger, secure a loop of cord to back of Angel.

NOTE: Cut ribbon in half.

3: Holding ribbons together, tie into a bow; trim ends. Glue lace, bows and ribbon roses to Hanger as shown in photo.❈

TECHNIQUE:
• Plastic Canvas

SIZE:
• Angel is 3½" x 4½"
• Hanger is 3¼" x 4½", not including lace

MATERIALS:
• ½ sheet of 7-count plastic canvas
• 10" white 1½" pre-gathered lace
• ⅔ yd. pink ¼" picot-edged satin ribbon
• One mauve ½" and one lt. pink ¼" ribbon rose
• Craft glue or glue gun
• Metallic cord (for amount see Color Key on page 27)
• Pearlized cord (for amount see Color Key)
• Worsted-weight or plastic canvas yarn (for amounts see Color Key)

Petite Samplers

Designed by Celia Lange Designs

TECHNIQUE:
• Cross Stitch

MATERIALS FOR ONE:
• Two 8" x 9" pieces of white 14-count Aida
• White floss
• Polyester fiberfill

STITCHING INSTRUCTIONS

NOTE: Graphs continued on pages 18 and 19.

1: Center and stitch design of choice, using two strands floss for Cross Stitch. Use two strands floss for Backstitch of border and straight lines on #3 and #5, Backstitch of letters and borders on #4 and Backstitch of border on #6. Use one strand floss for remaining Backstitch and French Knots.

2: Trim stitched Aida 1" from design edges. Cut remaining piece of Aida same as stitched Aida. Holding pieces wrong sides together and working through both thicknesses, using white floss, Cross Stitch pieces together ½" from edges, inserting polyester fiberfill before closing last edge. For fringe, pull out fabric threads beyond stitching.❋

Sampler #1

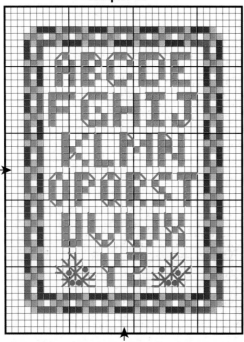

Sampler #3

Sampler #1

X	B'st	Fr	DMC	ANCHOR	J.&P. COATS	COLORS
■			#321	#47	#3500	Cherry Red
■			#367	#217	#6018	Pistachio Green Dk.
		◉	#666	#46	#3046	Geranium Dk.
■			#783	#307	#5307	Topaz Very Dk.
■	◢		#814	#45	#3044	Garnet Very Dk.
■	◢		#3815	#216	#6876	Celdon Green Dk.

Sampler #3

X	B'st	DMC	ANCHOR	J.&P. COATS	COLORS
	◢	#321	#47	#3500	Cherry Red
■		#666	#46	#3046	Geranium Dk.
	◢	#782	#308	#5308	Russet
	◢	#987	#245	#6258	Willow Green Dk.
■		#988	#243	#6266	Willow Green Med.
□		#3820	#306	#5363	Golden Wheat Dk.

Sampler #1 & #3
Stitch Count:
31 wide x 43 high

Approximate Design Size:
11-count 2⅞" x 4"
14-count 2¼" x 3⅛"
16-count 2" x 2¾"
18-count 1¾" x 2⅜"
22-count 1½" x 2"

Petite Samplers Instructions on page 16

Sampler #2

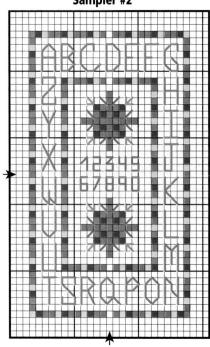

Sampler #2
Stitch Count:
25 wide x 43 high

Approximate Design Size:
11-count 2⅜" x 4"
14-count 1⅞" x 3⅛"
16-count 1⅝" x 2¾"
18-count 1⅜" x 2⅜"
22-count 1⅛" x 2"

Sampler #4

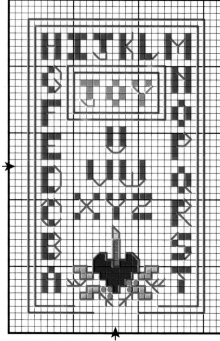

Sampler #4
Stitch Count:
27 wide x 44 high

Approximate Design Size:
11-count 2½" x 4"
14-count 2" x 3¼"
16-count 1¾" x 2¾"
18-count 1½" x 2½"
22-count 1¼" x 2"

Sampler #2

X	B'st	DMC	ANCHOR	J.&P. COATS	COLORS
	⟋	#321	#47	#3500	Cherry Red
◻		#367	#217	#6018	Pistachio Green Dk.
◻		#782	#308	#5308	Russet
◼		#814	#45	#3044	Garnet Very Dk.
	⟋	#988	#243	#6258	Willow Green Med.
◻	⟋	#3820	#306	#5363	Golden Wheat Dk.

Sampler #4

X	B'st	¾x	Fr	DMC	ANCHOR	J.&P. COATS	COLORS
◼		◣		#321	#47	#3500	Cherry Red
	⟋			#552	#94	#4092	Violet Dk.
◻				#553	#92	#4097	Violet Med.
◻	⟋		●	#666	#46	#3046	Geranium Dk.
◻			◻	#725	#305	#2294	Topaz Med.
	⟋			#814	#45	#3044	Garnet Very Dk.
	⟋			#986	#246	#6021	Pistachio Green Ultra Dk.
◼	⟋			#987	#245	#6258	Willow Green Dk.
◻				#988	#243	#6266	Willow Green Med.
	⟋			#3820	#306	#5363	Golden Wheat Dk.

Sampler #5
Stitch Count:
31 wide x 45 high

Approximate Design Size:
11-count 2⅞" x 4⅛"
14-count 2¼" x 3¼"
16-count 2" x 2⅞"
18-count 1¾" x 2½"
22-count 1½" x 2⅛"

Sampler #5

Sampler #5

X	B'st	Fr	DMC	ANCHOR	J.&P. COATS	COLORS
	⟋		#321	#47	#3500	Cherry Red
		●	#666	#46	#3046	Geranium Dk.
	⟋		#782	#308	#5308	Russet
	⟋		#987	#245	#6258	Willow Green Dk.
◻			#988	#243	#6266	Willow Green Med.

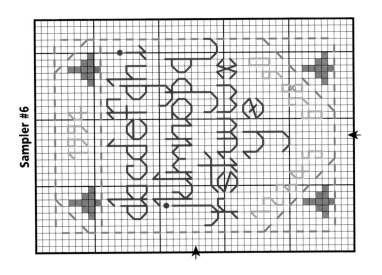

Sampler #6
Stitch Count:
29 wide x 43 high

Approximate Design Size:
11-count 2⅝" x 4"
14-count 2⅛" x 3⅛"
16-count 1⅞" x 2¾"
18-count 1⅝" x 2⅜"
22-count 1⅜" x 2"

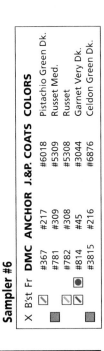

X	B'st	Fr	DMC	ANCHOR	J.&P. COATS	COLORS
▨			#367	#217	#6018	Pistachio Green Dk.
▨		▨	#781	#309	#5309	Russet Med.
▨			#782	#308	#5308	Russet
■		◙	#814	#45	#3044	Garnet Very Dk.
■			#3815	#216	#6876	Celdon Green Dk.

Golden Lace Globes Continued from page 13

sp, ch 3) around, join, fasten off (40 dc, 20 ch sps).

NOTE: For **picot,** ch 3, sl st in top of last st made.

Rnd 8: Join metallic thread in any ch sp, ch 3, 2 dc in same sp, dc in next st, picot, dc in next st, (3 dc in next ch sp, dc in next st, picot, dc in next st) around, join, fasten off.

Rnd 9: Join red with with sl st in any picot, ch 2, hdc in same sp, ch 3, (2 hdc in next picot, ch 3) around, join with sl st in top of ch-2.

Rnds 10-15: Repeat rnds 6-9 consecutively, ending with rnd 7. At end of last rnd, **do not** fasten off.

Rnds 16-23: Ch 3, dc in next st, ch 3, (dc in each of next 2 dc, ch 3) around, join.

Rnd 24: Ch 3, dc in next st, ch 6, sl st in 4th ch from hook, ch 2, (dc in each of next 2 dc, ch 6, sl st in 4th ch from hook, ch 2) around, join, fasten off.

FINISHING

1: For **hanger,** cut 6" piece of red ribbon. Insert one end through hanger at top of plastic ornament; tie ends into a knot.

2: Cut remaining red ribbon in half. With both pieces held together, weave through ch sps of rnd 16. Insert plastic ornament, pull ribbon

ends to gather around ball, tie ends into a bow.

ORNAMENT NO. 3
COVER

Rnds 1-3: With white, work same rnds of Ornament No. 1.

Rnd 4: Beg shell, ch 5, (shell in next shell, ch 5) around, join.

NOTE: For **picot,** ch 3, sl st in top of last st made.

Rnd 5: Sl st in next st, (sl st, ch 3, dc, picot, ch 1, dc, picot, dc) in next ch sp, (2 dc, picot, ch 1, dc, picot, dc) in 3rd ch of each ch-5 and in each shell around, join.

Rnd 6: Working behind picot, sl st in next st, sl st in next ch-1 sp, ch 6, sl st in 3rd ch from hook, dc in same sp, ch 3, (dc, picot, dc, ch 3) in each ch-1 sp around, join with sl st in 3rd ch of ch-6.

NOTE: For **picot shell,** (3 dc, picot, ch 1, dc, picot, 2 dc) in next ch sp.

Rnd 7: Sl st in next dc, (sl st, ch 3, 2 dc, picot, ch 1, dc, picot, 2 dc) in next ch sp, (3 dc, picot, ch 1, dc, picot, 2 dc) in each ch-3 sp around, join with sl st in top of ch-3, fasten off.

Rnd 8: Join dk. green with sl st in any ch-1 sp, ch 6, sl st in 3rd ch from hook, dc in same sp, ch 4, *(dc, picot, dc) in next ch-1 sp, ch 4; repeat from * around, join with sl st in 3rd ch of ch-6, fasten off.

Rnd 9: Join white with sl st in

any ch-4 sp, (ch 3, 2 dc, picot, ch 1, dc, picot, 2 dc) in same sp, picot shell in each ch-4 sp around, join with sl st in top of ch-3, fasten off.

Rnds 10-22: Working in color sequence of metallic thread/white, red/white, metallic thread/white, dk. green/white, repeat rnds 8 and 9 alternately, ending with rnd 8 and green.

Rnd 23: Join white with sl st in any ch-4 sp, (ch 3, 2 dc, ch 1, 3 dc) in same ch sp, (3 dc, ch 1, 3 dc) in each ch-4 sp around, join, fasten off.

Rnd 24: Join metallic thread with sc in any st, sc in each st and in each ch sp around, join with sl st in first sc, fasten off.

FINISHING

Work Ornament No. 2 Finishing.

ORNAMENT NO. 4
COVER

With lt. green, work same as Ornament No. 1.

FINISHING

1: For hanger, cut 6" piece of metallic thread. Insert one end through hanger at top of plastic ornament; tie ends into a knot.

2: Cut metallic cord in half. With both pieces held together, weave through ch sps of rnd 16. Insert plastic ornament, pull cord ends to gather around ball, tie ends into a bow.❈

19

Crystal Snowflakes

Designed by Katherine Eng

TECHNIQUE:
• Crochet

SIZE:
• Approximately 4½" across

MATERIALS FOR ONE:
• Speed-Cro-Sheen or size 3 crochet cotton — 30 yds. ecru
• 1 yd. ecru ¼" ribbon
• Crystal 8-mm round faceted beads — 24 each for No. 1 or No. 2, 18 for No. 3 and 20 for No. 4
• Embroidery needle
• C crochet hook or size needed to obtain gauge

GAUGE:
• 1 dc = ½" tall

SNOWFLAKE NO. 1

NOTE: With needle, thread amount of beads indicated in materials onto crochet cotton, push back along thread until needed. When beads are worked, push to right side of work.

Rnd 1: Ch 4, sl st in first ch to form ring, ch 1, 8 sc in ring, join with sl st in first sc (8 sc).

Rnd 2: Ch 1, sc in first st, ch 1, pull up one bead, ch 2, (sc in next st, ch 1, pull up one bead, ch 2) around, join.

Rnd 3: Ch 1, sc in first st, ch 3, (sc in next sc, ch 3) around, join.

Rnd 4: Ch 1, sc in first st, (2 dc, ch 2, 2 dc) in next ch-3 sp, *sc in next st, (2 dc, ch 2, 2 dc) in next ch-3 sp; repeat from * around, join.

Rnd 5: Ch 1, pull up one bead, sc in first st, *[sc in each of next 2 dc, (sc, ch 3, sc) in next ch sp, sc in each of next 2 dc], pull up one bead, sc in next st; repeat from * 6 more times; repeat between [ ], join.

Rnd 6: Ch 1, sc in first sc, *[ch 2, skip next 3 sts, (sc, ch 3, sc) in next ch sp, ch 2, skip next 3 sts], sc in next st; repeat from * 6 more times; repeat between [ ], join.

Rnd 7: Ch 1, sc in first st, *[2 sc in next ch-2 sp, sc in next st, (sc, ch 3, sc) in next ch-3 sp, sc in next st, 2 sc in next ch-2 sp], sc in next st; repeat from * 6 more times; repeat between [ ], join.

Rnd 8: Ch 1, (sc, ch 3, sc) in first st, *[ch 3, skip next 4 sts, (sc, ch 2, sc, ch 1, pull up one bead, ch 2, sc, ch 2, sc) in next ch-3 sp, ch 2, skip next 4 sts], (sc, ch 3, sc) in next st; repeat from * 6 more times; repeat between [ ], join, fasten off.

For **hanger,** tie ribbon to edge of Snowflake.

SNOWFLAKE NO. 2

Rnds 1-3: Work same rnds of Snow

flake No. 1.

Rnd 4: Ch 1, sc in first st, 3 sc in next ch-3 sp, (sc in next st, 3 sc in next ch-3 sp) around, join.

Rnd 5: Ch 1, sc in first sc, (ch 3, skip next st, sc in next st) around to last st; to **join,** ch 1, skip last st, hdc in first st (16 ch sps).

Rnd 6: Ch 1, sc around joining hdc, (2 dc, ch 3, 2 dc) in next ch sp, *sc in next ch sp, (2 dc, ch 3, 2 dc) in next ch sp; repeat from * around, join with sl st in first sc.

Rnd 7: Repeat rnd 5 of Snowflake No. 1.

Rnd 8: Ch 1, (sc, ch 3, sc) in first st, *[ch 3, skip next 3 sts, (sc, ch 2, pull up one bead, ch 3, sc) in next ch-3 sp, ch 3, skip next 3 sts], (sc, ch 3, sc) in next st; repeat from * 6 more times; repeat between [ ], join, fasten off.

For **hanger,** tie ribbon to edge of Snowflake.

SNOWFLAKE NO. 3

Rnd 1: Ch 6, sl st in first ch to form ring, ch 1, 12 sc in ring, join with sl st in first sc (12 sc).

Rnd 2: Ch 1, sc in first st, ch 3, skip next st, (sc in next st, ch 3, skip next st) around, join (6 sc, 6 ch sps).

Rnd 3: Ch 1, sc in first st, (sc, pull up one bead, 2 sc) in next ch sp, *sc in next st, (sc, pull up one bead, 2 sc) in next ch sp; repeat from * around, join (24 sc).

Rnd 4: Ch 1, sc in first st, (ch 3, skip next st, sc in next st) around to last st; to **join,** ch 1, skip last st, hdc in first st (12 sc, 12 ch sps).

NOTE: For **shell,** (3 dc, ch 3, 3 dc) in next ch sp.

Rnd 5: Ch 1, sc around joining hdc, shell in next ch sp, (sc in next ch sp, shell in next ch sp) around, join with sl st in first sc.

Rnd 6: (Ch 3, 2 dc, ch 3, 3 dc) in first st, ch 1, (sc, ch 3, sc) in ch sp of next shell, ch 1, *shell in next sc, ch 1, (sc, ch 3, sc) in ch sp of next shell, ch 1; repeat from * around, join with sl st in top of ch-3, **turn.**

Rnd 7: (Sl st, ch 1, sc) in next ch-1 sp, *[ch 1, (sc, ch 1, pull up one bead, ch 1, sc) in next ch-3 sp, ch 1, sc in next ch-1 sp, ch 2, (sc, ch 3, sc) in next shell, ch 2], sc in next ch-1 sp; repeat from * 4 more times; repeat between [ ], join with sl st in first sc, **turn.**

Rnd 8: (Sl st, ch 1, sc) in next ch-2 sp, *[ch 2, (sc, ch 1, pull up one bead, ch 1, sc) in next ch-3 sp, ch 2, sc in next ch-2 sp, ch 2, sc in next ch-1 sp, ch 6, skip next bead, sc in next ch-1 sp, ch 2], sc in next ch-2 sp; repeat from * 4 more times; repeat between [ ], join, fasten off.

For **hanger,** tie ribbon to edge of Snowflake.

SNOWFLAKE NO. 4

Rnd 1: Ch 4, sl st in first ch to form ring, ch 3, dc in ring, ch 2, (2 dc in ring, ch 3) 5 times, join with sl st in top of ch-3 (12 dc, 6 ch sps).

Rnd 2: Ch 3, sc in each dc and 3 sc in each ch sp around, join with sl st in first sc (30 sc).

Rnd 3: Ch 1, sc in first st, (ch 1, skip next st, sc in next st) around to last st; to **join,** ch 1, skip last st, hdc in first st (15 ch sps).

Rnd 4: Ch 1, sc around joining hdc, *[(ch 3, sc in next ch sp) 2 times, ch 2, pull up one bead, ch 3], sc in next ch sp; repeat from * 3 more times; repeat between [ ], join with sl st in first sc.

Rnd 5: (Sl st, ch 1, sc) in first ch sp, *[ch 2, pull up one bead, ch 3, sc in next ch sp, ch 3, sc in next ch sp before bead, ch 3, sc in same ch sp after bead, ch 3], sc in next ch sp; repeat from * 3 more times; repeat between [ ], join.

Rnd 6: (Sl st, ch 1, sc) in next ch sp before bead, ch 3, sc in same ch sp after bead, (2 dc, ch 2, 2 dc) in next ch sp, (sc, ch 3, sc) in next ch-3 sp, (2 dc, ch 2, 2 dc) in next ch sp, *sc in next ch sp before bead, ch 3, sc in same ch sp after bead, (2 dc, ch 2, 2 dc) in next ch sp, (sc, ch 3, sc) in next ch-3 sp, (2 dc, ch 2, 2 dc) in next ch sp; repeat from * around, join.

Rnd 7: Ch 1, *(sc, ch 3, sc) in next ch sp, sc in each of next 2 dc, (sc, ch 2, pull up one bead, ch 3, sc) in next ch sp, sc in each of next 2 dc; repeat from * around, join, fasten off.

For **hanger,** tie ribbon to edge of Snowflake.❋

Celebration Quilts

Designed by Carolyn Christmas

TECHNIQUE:
• Plastic Canvas

SIZE:
• Large Ornament is 3¼" square
• Each Medium Ornament is 3" square
• Small Ornament is 2⅝" square

MATERIALS FOR ONE OF EACH:
• ½ sheet of 7-count plastic canvas
• Metallic cord (for amount see Color Key)
• Worsted-weight or plastic canvas yarn (for amounts see Color Key)

CUTTING INSTRUCTIONS

NOTE: Graphs continued on page 26.

A: For Large Ornament, cut one 21 x 21 holes.

B: For Medium Ornaments #1-#4, cut four 19 x 19 holes.

C: For Small Ornament, cut one 17 x 17 holes.

STITCHING INSTRUCTIONS

1: Using colors and stitches indicated, work A-C pieces according to graphs; with gold cord, Overcast unfinished edges.

2: For hangers, secure a loop of cord to back of each Ornament as shown in photo.❈

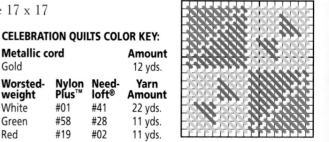

C – Small Ornament
(cut 1) 17 x 17 holes

CELEBRATION QUILTS COLOR KEY:

Metallic cord			Amount
☐ Gold			12 yds.

Worsted-weight	Nylon Plus™	Need-loft®	Yarn Amount
☐ White	#01	#41	22 yds.
■ Green	#58	#28	11 yds.
■ Red	#19	#02	11 yds.

Beaded Treasures

Designed by Carol Krob

CUTTING INSTRUCTIONS

A: For Beaded Ornaments #1-#4, cut one each from clear according to graphs.

B: For optional backings, cut one each from colored canvas according to A graphs.

STITCHING INSTRUCTIONS

1: For Beaded Ornaments, with thread, sew beads to each A according to graph; or, for floss ornaments, using six strands floss in colors indicated and French Knot, embroider A pieces according to graphs.

2: For optional backings, holding one unworked B to wrong side of each worked piece, with metallic ribbon or braid, Whipstitch together. For Ornaments without backings, Overcast unfinished edges.

3: Attach a small loop of ribbon or braid at top of each Ornament for hanger.❋

A – Beaded Ornament #1
(cut 1) 18 x 18 holes

A – Beaded Ornament #2
(cut 1) 18 x 18 holes

A – Beaded Ornament #3
(cut 1) 18 x 18 holes

A – Beaded Ornament #4
(cut 1) 18 x 18 holes

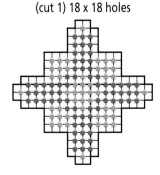

BEADED TREASURES COLOR KEY:

1/16" metallic ribbon or braid	**Amount**
☐ Gold	6 yds.

Seed beads or floss	**Amount**
Gold	181 beads or 7 yds.
Green	157 beads or 5 yds.
Red	146 beads or 5 yds.

STITCH KEY:

● Bead Attachment or French Knot

TECHNIQUE:
• Plastic Canvas

SIZE:
• Each is 1⅜" x 1⅜"

MATERIALS FOR ONE OF EACH:
• (NOTE: Ornaments may be beaded or stitched using floss and French Knot.)
• Scraps of clear 14-count plastic canvas
• Scraps of red or green 14-count plastic canvas (optional for backings)
• Beading needle and quilting thread (optional for beaded ornaments)
• 1/16" metallic ribbon or heavy metallic braid (for amount see Color Key)
• Seed beads or six-strand embroidery floss (for amounts see Color Key)

23

Gossamer Bells

Designed by Joan Glass

TECHNIQUE:
• Crochet

SIZE:
• Approximately 4" tall

MATERIALS FOR ONE:
• Size 10 bedspread cotton — 30 yds.
• 13-mm-diameter bead
• Liquid fabric stiffener
• 2¾"-tall glass measuring 1½" across bottom and 2½" across top
• Styrofoam® or cutting board
• Plastic wrap
• Tapestry needle
• No. 9 steel crochet hook or size needed to obtain gauge

GAUGE:
• 1 tr = ½" tall

BELL NO. 1

Rnd 1: Ch 6, sl st in first ch to form ring, ch 4, (dc in ring, ch 1) 11 times, join with sl st in 3rd ch of ch-4 (12 dc, 12 ch sps).

Rnd 2: Ch 5, (dc in next st, ch 2) around, join with sl st in 3rd ch of ch-5.

Rnd 3: Ch 3, 2 dc in next ch sp, (dc in next st, 2 dc in next ch sp) around, join with sl st in top of ch-3 (36 dc).

Rnd 4: Working this rnd in **back lps** only, ch 1, sc in each st around, join with sl st in first sc.

NOTES: For **beginning cluster (beg cl),** ch 4, *yo 2 times, insert hook in same st, yo, draw lp through, (yo, draw through 2 lps on hook) 2 times; repeat from *, yo, draw through all 3 lps on hook.

For **cluster (cl),** yo 2 times, insert hook in next st, yo, draw lp through, (yo, draw through 2 lps on hook) 2 times, *yo 2 times, insert hook in same st, yo, draw lp through, (yo, draw through 2 lps on hook) 2 times; repeat from *, yo, draw through all 4 lps on hook.

Rnd 5: Beg cl, ch 2, skip next 2 sts, (cl in next st, ch 2, skip next 2 sts) around, join with sl st in top of first cl (12 cls).

Rnd 6: Ch 1, sc in first st, (ch 6, sc in next cl) around; to **join,** ch 3, tr in first st.

Rnd 7: Ch 1, sc around joining tr, (ch 6, sc in next ch sp) around, join as before.

Rnd 8: Ch 1, sc around joining tr, ch 4, (sc in next ch sp, ch 4) around, join with sl st in first sc.

Rnd 9: Ch 2, hdc in each st and in each ch around, join with sl st in top of ch-2 (60 hdc).

Rnd 10: Beg cl, ch 5, skip next 4 sts, (cl in next st, ch 5, skip next 4 sts) around, join with sl st in top of first cl (12 cl).

Baby's First Christmas

Designed by Jocelyn Sass

TECHNIQUE:
• Crochet

SIZE:
• Each Shoe is 2½" long

MATERIALS:
• Pearlized metallic cord or worsted-weight yarn — 16 yds. pearl/blue and 2 yds. pearl/white
• 10" white ⅛" satin ribbon
• Two white ¼" satin ribbon roses
• Craft glue or hot glue gun
• E crochet hook or size needed to obtain gauge.

GAUGE:
• 5 sc = 1"
• 2 sc rows = ½"

SHOE (make 2)

NOTE: Do not join rnds unless otherwise stated. Mark first st of each rnd.

Rnd 1: With pearl/blue, ch 8, 2 sc in 2nd ch from hook, sc in next 5 chs; for **toe,** 5 sc in last ch; working on opposite side of ch, sc in next 5 chs, 2 sc in last ch (19 sc).

Rnd 2: 2 sc in first st, sc in next 6 sts, hdc in next st, 2 hdc in each of next 3 sts, hdc in next st, sc in next 6 sts, 2 sc in last st (16 sc, 8 hdc).

Rnd 3: Working this rnd in **back lps** only, sc in each st around, join with sl st in first sc (24 sc).

Rnd 4: Ch 1, sc in each st around, join.

Rnd 5: Ch 1, sc in first 4 sts, (dc next 2 sts tog) 3 times, dc in next st, (dc next 2 sts tog) 3 times, sc in last 7 sts, join, fasten off (11 sc, 7 dc).

Rnd 6: With toe pointing to the left, working in **front lps** only, join pearl/white with sl st in center st on side of Shoe, (ch 1, sl st in next st) 8 times, for **strap,** ch 5, join with sl st in first sl st, fasten off.

Glue one end of ribbon to inside of each heel and one ribbon rose to outside edge of each Shoe at end of strap as shown in photo.❀

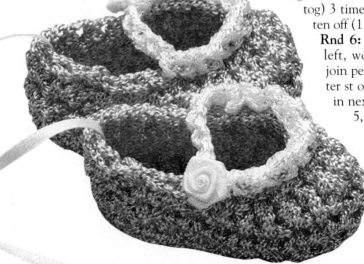

Rnd 11: Ch 1, sc in first st, (ch 4, sc in next ch-3 sp, ch 4, sc in next cl) around to last ch sp, ch 4, sc in last ch sp; to **join,** ch 2, hdc in first st.

Rnds 12-13: Ch 1, sc around joining hdc, (ch 4, sc in next ch sp) around, join as before.

Rnd 14: Ch 1, sc around joining hdc, ch 4, (sc in next ch sp, ch 4) around, join with sl st in first sc, fasten off.

CLAPPER

Rnd 1: Ch 4, 6 dc in 4th ch from hook, join with sl st in top of ch-3 (7 dc).

Rnd 2: Ch 3, dc in same st, 2 dc in each st around, join (14). Insert bead.

Rnd 3: Ch 3, skip next st, (dc next 2 sts tog) around, join; ch for 2½", fasten off leaving 6" end.

Tack opening at top of rnd 3 closed.

FINISHING

1: For **handle,** join with sl st on one side of rnd 1, ch 12, sl st on opposite side of rnd 1, **turn,** ch 1, 18 sc in ch-12 sp, join with sl st in first sl st, fasten off.

2: Wrap glass with plastic wrap. Apply fabric stiffener to Bell according to manufacturer's instructions and place over glass. Place on foam or cutting board, pin every other ch sp on last rnd into a point. Let dry completely, shaping handle as it dries as shown in photo.

3: Pull 6" end on clapper from inside through center top of Bell, tie around handle to secure.

BELL NO. 2

Rnds 1-3: Work same rnds of Bell No. 1.

Rnd 4: (Ch 4, 2 tr, ch 3, 3 tr) in first st, skip next 5 sts, *(3 tr, ch 3, 3 tr) in next st, skip next 5 sts; repeat from * around, join with sl st in top of ch-4.

Rnd 5: Sl st in each of next 2 sts, (sl st, ch 4, 2 tr, ch 3, 3 tr) in next ch sp, (3 tr, ch 3, 3 tr) in each ch sp around, join.

NOTE: For **shell,** (2 tr, ch 3, 2 tr) in next ch sp.

For **beginning shell (beg shell),** sl st in next st, (sl st, ch 4, tr, ch 3, 2 tr) in next ch sp.

Rnd 6: Sl st in each of next 2 sts, (sl st, ch 4, tr, ch 3, 2 tr) in next ch sp, ch 3, sc in sp between next 2 3-tr groups, ch 3, (shell in next ch sp, ch 3, sc in sp between next 2 3-tr groups, ch 3) around, join.

Rnd 7: Beg shell, ch 3, (shell in ch sp of
Continued on page 26

Gossamer Bells Continued from page 25

next shell, ch 3) around, join.

Rnd 8: Beg shell, ch 3, sc in next ch sp, ch 3, (shell in next shell, ch 3, sc in next ch sp, ch 3) around, join.

Rnd 9: Beg shell, ch 4, sc in next sc, ch 4, (shell in next shell, ch 4, sc in next sc, ch 4) around, join.

NOTE: For **picot**, ch 4, sl st in 4th ch from hook.

Rnd 10: Ch 4, *[tr in next st, picot, (2 tr, ch 1, picot, ch 1, 2 tr) in next ch sp, tr in next st, picot], tr in each of next 2 sts; repeat from * 4 more times; repeat between [ ], tr in last st, join with sl st in top of ch-4, fasten off.

CLAPPER

Work same as Bell No. 1 Clapper.

FINISHING

1: Work Step 1 of Bell No. 1.

2: Wrap glass with plastic wrap. Apply fabric stiffener to Bell according to manufacturer's instructions and place over glass. Let dry completely shaping handle as it dries as shown in photo.

3: Work Step 3 of Bell No. 1.

BELL NO. 3

Rnds 1-3: Work same rnds of Bell No. 1.

NOTE: For **picot,** ch 6, hdc in 3rd ch from hook, ch 2, sl st in base of last hdc, ch 3.

Rnd 4: Ch 1, sc in first st, *picot, skip next 2 sts, sc in next st; repeat from * 10 more times, picot, join with sl st in first ch of first picot (12 picots).

Rnd 5: Ch 6, sc in top of next picot, ch 2, (tr in next sc, ch 2, sc in top of next picot, ch 2) around, join with sl st in 4th ch of ch-6.

Rnd 6: Sl st in each of next 2 chs, (sl st, ch 1, sc) in next st, (ch 3, sc in next sc) around; to **join,** ch 1, dc in first sc.

Rnds 7-9: Ch 1, sc around joining dc, (ch 4, sc in next ch sp) around; to **join,** ch 2, dc in first sc.

Rnd 10: Ch 1, sc around joining dc, picot, (sc in next ch sp, picot)

around, join with sl st in first sc.

Rnd 11: Ch 7, sc in next picot, ch 3, (tr in next sc, ch 3, sc in next picot, ch 3) around, join with sl st in 4th ch of ch-7.

Rnd 12: Sl st in each of next 3 chs, (sl st, ch 1, sc) in next st, (ch 5, sc in next sc) around; to **join,** ch 3, dc in first sc.

Rnd 13: Ch 1, sc around joining dc, (ch 5, sc in next ch sp) around, join as before.

Rnd 14: Ch 1, sc around joining

dc, ch 3, hdc in 3rd ch from hook, ch 2, sl st in base of last hdc, ch 5, (sc in next ch sp, ch 3, hdc in 3rd ch from hook, ch 2, sl st in base of last hdc, ch 5) around, join with sl st in first sc, fasten off.

CLAPPER

Work same as Bell No. 1 Clapper.

FINISHING

Work same as Bell No. 2 Finishing.✤

Celebration Quilts

Instructions on page 22

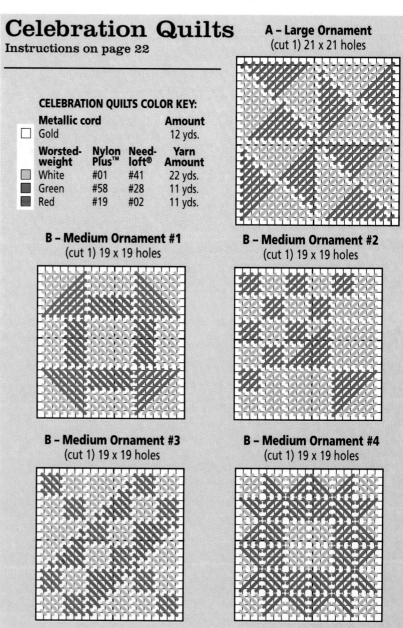

CELEBRATION QUILTS COLOR KEY:

Metallic cord			Amount
☐ Gold			12 yds.

Worsted-weight	Nylon Plus™	Need-loft®	Yarn Amount
☐ White	#01	#41	22 yds.
■ Green	#58	#28	11 yds.
▨ Red	#19	#02	11 yds.

A – Large Ornament
(cut 1) 21 x 21 holes

B – Medium Ornament #1
(cut 1) 19 x 19 holes

B – Medium Ornament #2
(cut 1) 19 x 19 holes

B – Medium Ornament #3
(cut 1) 19 x 19 holes

B – Medium Ornament #4
(cut 1) 19 x 19 holes

Victorian Trinkets Instructions on page 15

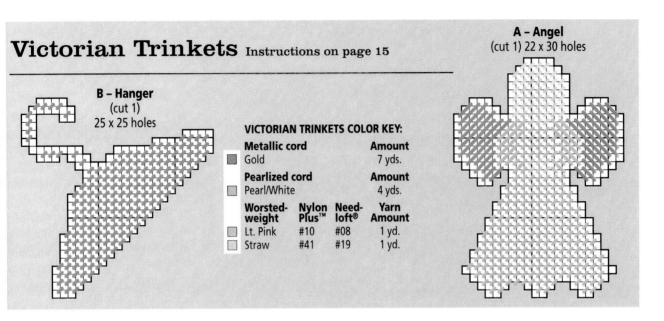

B – Hanger
(cut 1)
25 x 25 holes

A – Angel
(cut 1) 22 x 30 holes

VICTORIAN TRINKETS COLOR KEY:

Metallic cord			Amount
Gold			7 yds.

Pearlized cord			Amount
Pearl/White			4 yds.

Worsted-weight	Nylon Plus™	Need-loft®	Yarn Amount
Lt. Pink	#10	#08	1 yd.
Straw	#41	#19	1 yd.

Tiny Additions Instructions on page 14

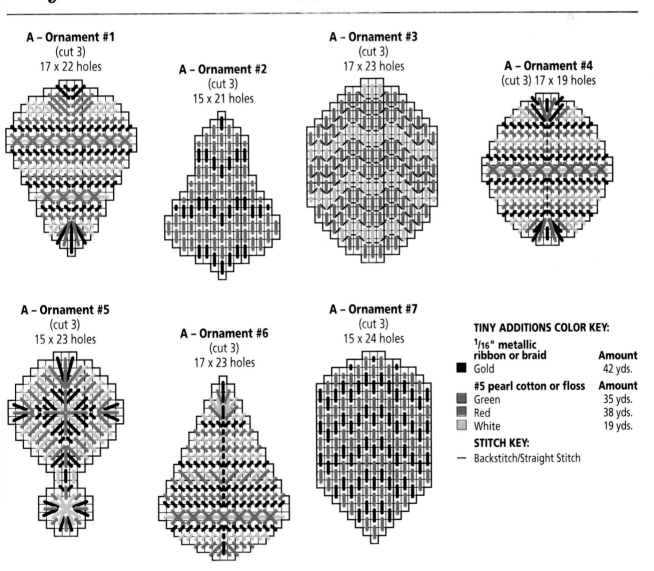

A – Ornament #1
(cut 3)
17 x 22 holes

A – Ornament #2
(cut 3)
15 x 21 holes

A – Ornament #3
(cut 3)
17 x 23 holes

A – Ornament #4
(cut 3) 17 x 19 holes

A – Ornament #5
(cut 3)
15 x 23 holes

A – Ornament #6
(cut 3)
17 x 23 holes

A – Ornament #7
(cut 3)
15 x 24 holes

TINY ADDITIONS COLOR KEY:

1/16" metallic ribbon or braid	Amount
Gold	42 yds.

#5 pearl cotton or floss	Amount
Green	35 yds.
Red	38 yds.
White	19 yds.

STITCH KEY:
— Backstitch/Straight Stitch

27

A *Joyous* Welcome

No holiday tradition is as universal as that of entertaining family and friends, and nothing adds warmth and charm to a holiday home like cheerful handmade decorations. From crocheted pillows that spell "joy" and beautifully appliquéd table linens to lace-trimmed hand towels and a personalized bell pull, these cheerful creations will fill your rooms with a bright, festive glow guaranteed to put smiles on everyone's faces.

Sweets for the Chef

Designed by Lois Winston

INSTRUCTIONS

NOTE: Pre-wash apron and print fabrics to remove sizing.

1: Trace Gingerbread House pattern pieces onto paper side of Wonder Under®. Apply Wonder Under® to wrong side of print fabrics, using red for door, pink for heart, lt. brown for house and chimney, lt. blue for windows, white for candy canes, roof and top of chimney, fabric for wreath and one gumdrop, yellow, orange and purple each for one gumdrop. Cut out pieces; peel off paper backing.

2: Position and center pieces on front of apron as shown in photo and according to pattern. Fuse in place following manufacturer's instructions.

3: Cut piece of Stitch-n-Tear® slightly larger than fused design. Pin to wrong side of apron under fused design. With white thread for windows, red thread for candy cane stripes and brown thread for house and with matching thread for remaining pieces, using a buttonhole stitch, machine appliqué along all raw edges of fused design pieces. Remove Stitch-n-Tear® following manufacturer's instructions.

4: Glue gems to roof and top of chimney as shown in photo. Tie ribbon into small bow; trim ends and glue to wreath as shown.✿

TECHNIQUE:
• Appliqué

MATERIALS:
• Full length red apron with green trim
• Small scraps of red, yellow, orange, pink, purple, lt. brown, lt. blue, green and white print fabrics
• ⅛ yd. red ⅛" satin ribbon
• 9" x 12" piece of Wonder Under®
• 8" x 9" piece of Stitch-n-Tear®
• Sewing thread to match fabric colors
• Sixteen multi-colored 6.5-mm round gems
• Tracing paper
• Craft glue

Gingerbread House Pattern

Welcome Accents

Designed by Jacquelyn Fox

TECHNIQUE:
• Cross Stitch & Sewing

MATERIALS:
• One 9" x 16" and two 6" x 30" pieces of white 28-count Jubilee
• ½ yd. fabric
• 1¼ yds. of 4-mm. twisted cord
• 1⅛ yds. of ¼" satin ribbon
• Craft batting
• Thread
• Craft glue

STITCHING INSTRUCTIONS

NOTE: For pillow borders, chart motifs from graph onto graph paper for proper border placement (see photo). Graphs and diagram on page 42.

1: Choosing correct letters and numbers from "Alphabet & Numbers" graph, center and stitch "Bell Pull" design onto 9" x 16" piece of Jubilee, stitching over two threads and using two strands floss for Cross Stitch and one strand floss for Backstitch and French Knots.

2: For bell pull front, trim stitched Jubilee to 6¾" wide x 14" tall forming pointed bottom as shown in photo. From fabric, cut two 1¾" x 12" pieces for side borders, two 1¾" x 7½" pieces for bottom borders and one 1¾" x 6" piece for top border. With right sides together and ¼" seams stitch borders to stitched Jubilee according to Border Mitering Placement Diagram (on page 42), mitering corners. Trims seams; press.

3: For back, from fabric, cut one same size as front. From batting, cut one piece same as front. Baste batting to wrong side of front.

With right sides together and ¼" seams, stitch back to front, leaving an opening. Turn right side out; press. Slip stitch opening closed. Stitch in the ditch around stitched Jubilee.

4: Glue twisted cord around stitched Jubilee edges and tie in bow as shown. From ribbon, cut two 2½" pieces for hanging loops. Cut remaining ribbon in half. Fold 2½" ribbon pieces in half and tack to top corners. Tie each remaining ribbon piece into a bow and tack to top corner as shown.

5: For pillow borders, center and stitch motif of choice onto each 6" x 30" piece of Jubilee, repeating design across to make a 24" length, stitching over two threads and using two strands floss for Cross Stitch and one strand floss for Backstitch and French Knots.

6: For each pillow border, trim stitched Jubilee piece to 6½" x 27". With right sides together and ¼" seams, stitch long edges together. Turn right side out; press. Turn under ¼" on each long edge of stitched Jubilee. Center and stitch Jubilee on top of fabric strip.✿

JOY Pillows

Designed by Michele Wilcox

TECHNIQUE:
• Crochet

SIZE:
• Each Pillow is approximately 7½" x 11½"

MATERIALS:
• Worsted-weight yarn — 3 oz. each red, green and white
• Polyester fiberfill
• Tapestry needle
• G crochet hook or size needed to obtain gauge

GAUGE:
• 4 sc = 1"
• 4 sc rows = 1"

"J" PILLOW SIDE (make 2)

Row 1: Starting at bottom, with red, ch 15, sc in 2nd ch from hook, sc in each ch across, turn (14 sc).

Rows 2-10: Ch 1, 2 sc in first st, sc in each st across with 2 sc in last st, turn, ending with 32 sts in last row.

Rows 11-16: Ch 1, sc in each st across, turn.

Row 17: For **first side,** ch 1, sc in first 12 sts, sc next 2 sts tog leaving remaining sts unworked, turn (13).

Row 18: Ch 1, sc first 2 sts tog, sc in each st across, turn (12).

Rows 19-23: Ch 1, sc in each st across, turn.

Row 24: Ch 1, 2 sc in first st, sc in next 9 sts, sc last 2 sts tog, turn (12).

Row 25: Ch 1, sc in each st across, turn.

Rows 26-28: Ch 1, sc first 2 sts tog, sc in each st across to last 2 sts, sc last 2 sts tog, turn, ending with 6 sc in last row. At end of last row, fasten off.

Row 17: For **second side,** skip next 4 unworked sts on row 16, join with sl st in next st, ch 1, sc next 2 sts tog, sc in each st across, turn (12 sc).

Rows 18-35: Ch 1, sc in each st across, turn.

Row 36: Ch 1, 2 sc in first st, sc in each st across with 2 sc in last st, turn, fasten off (14).

Row 37: With red, ch 7, join with sc in first st, sc in each st across, ch 8, turn.

Row 38: Sc in 2nd ch from hook, sc in each ch and in each st across, turn (28).

Row 39: Repeat row 36 (30).

Rows 40-50: Ch 1, sc in each st across, turn.

Row 51: Ch 1, sc first 2 sts tog, sc in each st across to last 2 sts, sc last 2 sts tog; for **first Pillow Side,** turn; for **second Pillow Side, do not** turn (28).

Rnd 52: Working around outer edge in sts and in ends of rows, ch 1, sc in each st and in each row around with 3 sc in each upper corner, join with sl st in first sc, fasten off.

"O" PILLOW SIDE (make 2)

Rows 1-16: With white, repeat same rows of "J" Pillow Side.

Row 17: For **first side,** ch 1, sc in first 12 sts, sc next 2 sts tog leaving remaining sts unworked, turn (13).

Row 18: Ch 1, sc first 2 sts tog, sc in each st across, turn (12).

Rows 19-33: Ch 1, sc in each st across, turn.

Row 34: Ch 1, 2 sc in first st, sc in each st

across, turn (13).

Row 35: Ch 1, sc in each st across with 2 sc in last st, **do not** turn, fasten off (14).

Row 17: For **second side,** skip next 4 unworked sts on row 16, join white with sl st in next st, ch 1, sc next 2 sts tog, sc in each st across, turn (12 sc).

Rows 18-33: Ch 1, sc in each st across, turn.

Row 34: Ch 1, sc in each st across with 2 sc in last st, turn (13).

Row 35: Ch 1, 2 sc in first st, sc in each st across, turn (14 sc).

Row 36: Ch 1, sc in each st across, ch 4, sc in each st across row 35 of

first side, turn (28 sc, 4 chs).

Row 37: Ch 1, sc in each st and in each ch across, turn (32).

Rows 38-41: Ch 1, sc in each st across, turn.

Rows 42-50: Ch 1, sc first 2 sts tog, sc in each st across to last 2 sts, sc last 2 sts tog, turn, ending with 14 sts in last row.

Row 51: Ch 1, sc in each st across, turn.

Rnd 52: Working around outer edge in sts and in ends of rows, ch 1, sc in each st and in each row around, join with sl st in first sc, fasten off.

Rnd 53: With right side facing you, working in ends of rows and in sts on inside edge, join with sc in any row, sc in each row and in each st around, join, fasten off.

LEAF (make 2)

With green, ch 9, sc in 2nd ch from hook, *(hdc, dc) in next ch, ch 2, sl st in next ch, sc in next ch; repeat from *, (hdc, 2 dc, ch 2, 2 dc, hdc) in last ch; working on opposite side of ch, [sc in next ch, sl st in next ch, ch 2, (dc, hdc) in next ch]; repeat between [ ], sc in last ch, fasten off.

BERRY (make 2)

Rnd 1: With red, ch 2, 6 sc in 2nd ch from hook, **do not** join (6 sc).

Rnd 2: Sc in each st around; leaving 8" for sewing, fasten off.

For front, sew Leaves and Berries to one Pillow Side as shown in photo.

"Y" PILLOW SIDE (make 2)

Row 1: With green, ch 11, sc in 2nd ch from hook, sc in each ch across, turn (10 sc).

Row 2: Ch 1, 2 sc in first st, sc in each st across with 2 sc in last st, turn (12 sc).

Rows 3-24: Ch 1, sc in each st across, turn.

Rows 25-30: Repeat row 2, ending with 24 sts in last row.

Row 31: For **first side,** ch 1, 2 sc in first st, sc in next 9 sts, sc next 2 sts tog leaving remaining sts unworked, turn (12).

Row 32: Ch 1, sc first 2 sts tog, sc in each st across with 2 sc in last st, turn.

Row 33: Ch 1, sc in each st across, turn.

Row 34: Repeat row 32.

Row 35: Ch 1, 2 sc in first st, sc in next 9 sts, sc last 2 sts tog, turn.

Rows 36-39: Repeat rows 32 and 35 alternately.

Rows 40-50: Ch 1, sc in each st across, turn.

Row 51: Ch 1, sc first 2 sts tog, sc in each st across to last 2 sts, sc last 2 sts tog, fasten off (10).

Row 31: For **second side,** join green with sl st in next unworked st

on row 30, ch 1, sc same st and next st tog, sc in each st across with 2 sc in last st, turn (12 sc).

Row 32: Ch 1, 2 sc in first st, sc in next 9 sts, sc last 2 sts tog, turn.

Row 33: Ch 1, sc in each st across, turn.

Rows 34-39: Repeat rows 35 and 32 of first side alternately.

Rows 40-51: Repeat same rows of first side. At end of last row, **do not** fasten off, turn.

Rnd 52: Working around outer edge in sts and in ends of rows, ch 1, sc in each st and in each row around with 3 sc in each corner, join with sl st in first sc, fasten off.

ASSEMBLY

For each Pillow, hold Pillow Sides wrong sides together, matching sts; with matching color, sew together through **back lps,** stuffing before closing.❊

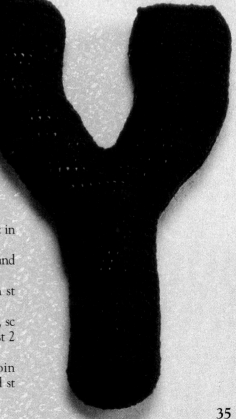

Angelic Silhouette

Designed by Bonnie J. Crawford

TECHNIQUE:
• Crochet

SIZE:
• Angel is 4¾" tall
• Edging is ¾" wide x 16"long

MATERIALS FOR ONE:
• Size 10 bedspread cotton — 150 yds. white
• 16" x 25" hand towel
• White sewing thread
• Sewing needle
• C crochet hook or size needed to obtain gauge

GAUGE:
• 7sc = 1"
• dc = ⅜" tall

ANGEL

NOTE: Do not join rnds unless otherwise stated. Mark first st of each rnd.

Rnd 1: Starting at **head,** ch 2, 7 sc in 2nd ch from hook (7 sc).

Rnd 2: 2 sc in each st around (14).

Rnd 3: (2 sc in next st, sc in next st) around, join (21).

Rnd 4: (2 sc in next st, sc in each of next 2 sts) around, join with sl st in first sc (28).

Row 5: Working in rows, ch 1, sc in first 5 sts leaving remaining sts unworked, turn (5 sc).

Row 6: For **first wing,** ch 3, 4 dc in same st leaving remaining sts unworked, turn (5 dc).

Row 7: Ch 4, dc in next st, (ch 1, dc in next st) across, turn.

Row 8: Ch 1, sc in each st and in each ch sp across to ch-4, sc in ch-4 sp, sc in 3rd ch of ch-4, turn (9 sc).

Row 9: Ch 5, skip next st, dc in next st, (ch 2, skip next st, dc in next st) across, turn.

Row 10: Ch 1, sc in each st and 2 sc in each ch sp across to ch-5, 2 sc in ch-5 sp, sc in 3rd ch of ch-5, turn (13 sc).

Row 11: Ch 6, skip next 2 sts, dc in next st, (ch 3, skip next 2 sts, dc in next st) across, turn.

Row 12: Ch 1, sc in each st and 3 sc in each ch sp across to ch-6, 3 sc in ch-6 sp, sc in 3rd ch of ch-6, turn, fasten off (17 sc).

Row 6: For **second wing,** with wrong side row 5 facing you, join with sl st in last st, ch 4, 4 dc in same st, turn (5 dc).

Rows 7-12: Repeat same rows of first wing.

Row 13: For **hair,** working in unworked sts of rnd 4, join with sc in 4th st, (ch 3, sc in next st) 16 times, fasten off.

Row 14: For **body,** with right side of row 5 facing you, join with sl st in first unworked st, ch 3, dc in same st, 2 dc in each of next 2 sts, turn (6 dc).

Continued on page 43

Company's Coming

Designed by Elizabeth A. White

SNOWFLAKE

NOTES: For **small cluster (sm cl),** *yo 2 times, insert hook in ring or ch sp, yo, draw lp through, (yo, draw through 2 lps on hook) 2 times; repeat from * in ring or same ch sp, yo, draw through all 3 lps on hook.

For **large cluster (lg cl),** *yo 2 times, insert hook in ring, yo, draw through ring, (yo, draw through 2 lps on hook) 2 times; repeat from * 2 more times, yo, draw through all 4 lps on hook.

Rnd 1: Ch 4, sl st in first ch to form ring, ch 4, sm cl, ch 4, (lg cl, ch 4) 5 times, join with sl st in top of first cl (6 cls, 6 ch sps).

Rnd 2: Ch 1, sc in first st, ch 4, sc in next ch sp, ch 4, (sc in next st, ch 4, sc in next ch sp, ch 4) around, join with sl st in frst sc (12 sc, 12 ch sps).

Rnd 3: Sl st in each of next 2 chs, ch 1, sc in same ch sp, ch 6, (sc in next ch sp, ch 6) around, join.

Rnd 4: Ch 1, (4 sc, ch 3, 4 sc) in each ch sp around, join.

Rnd 5: Sl st in each of next 3 sts, (sl st, ch 1, sc) in next ch sp, *[ch 3, (sm cl, ch 3, sm cl, ch 8, sm cl, ch 3, sm cl) in next ch sp, ch 3], sc in next ch sp; repeat from * 4 more times; repeat between [ ], join.

Rnd 6: Sl st in next ch sp, ch 1, (2 sc, ch 3, 2 sc) in same ch sp, (2 sc, ch 3, 2 sc) in each ch-3 sp around with (5 sc, ch 3, 5 sc) in each ch-8 sp, join, fasten off.

WREATH

Rnd 1: Ch 50, sl st in first ch to form
Continued on page 43

TECHNIQUE:
• Crochet

SIZE:
• Snowflake is 4" across
• Wreath is 4¾" across
• Edging is 1¼" wide x 16" long

MATERIALS FOR ONE:
• Size 10 bedspread cotton — 200 yds. white
• 12" red ¼" ribbon (for Wreath)
• White sewing thread
• 16" x 25" hand towel
• Sewing needle
• No. 7 steel crochet hook or size needed to obtain gauge

GAUGE:
• 4 sc sts = ⅜"
• 4 shell rows = 1½"
• Rnd 1 of Snowflake is 1" across

French Horn Trio

Designed by Lois Winston

INSTRUCTIONS

NOTE: Pre-wash napkin, place mat, breadcover and print fabrics to remove sizing.

1: Trace appliqué pattern pieces onto paper side of Wonder Under®, tracing three flowers, three sets of leaves, three flower centers and three trumpets. Apply Wonder Under® to wrong side of print fabrics, using gold print for trumpets and flower centers, red print for flowers and green print for leaves. Cut out pieces; peel off paper backing.

2: Position pieces for napkin and breadcover diagonally in one corner and pieces for place mat at top left corner as shown in photo and according to pattern. Fuse in place following manufacturer's instructions.

3: Cut piece of Stitch-n-Tear® slightly larger than each fused design. Pin to wrong side of fabric under each fused design. With gold metallic thread and using a buttonhole stitch, machine appliqué along all stitching lines and raw edges of fused design pieces. Remove Stitch-n-Tear® following manufacturer's instructions.❈

TECHNIQUE:
- Appliqué

SIZE:
- Appliqué is 3⅛" x 5⅝"

MATERIALS:
- Teal napkin, place mat and breadcover
- Scraps of red, gold and green print fabrics
- 9" x 12" piece of Wonder Under®
- 7" x 15" piece of Stitch-n-Tear®
- Gold metallic sewing thread
- Pencil
- Iron
- Tracing paper

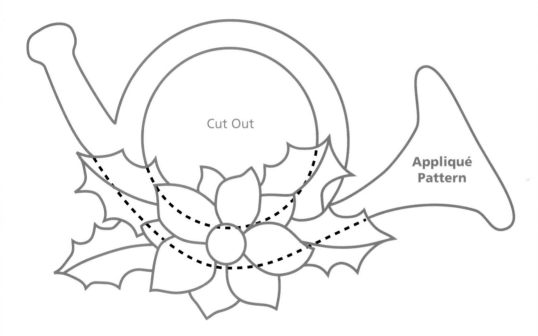

Cut Out

Appliqué Pattern

Blossoms in the Snow

Designed by Lucille LaFlamme

TECHNIQUE:
• Crochet

SIZE:
• 12" across

MATERIALS FOR ONE:
• Size 10 bedspread cotton — 100 yds. white
• 100 yds. red
• No.7 steel crochet hook or size needed to obtain gauge

GAUGE:
• Each Motif is 2" across

FIRST MOTIF

NOTE: For **picot,** ch 3, sl st in top of last st made.

Rnd 1: With red, ch 7, sl st in first ch to form ring, ch 1, (2 sc in ring, picot) 6 times, join with sl st in first sc (12 sc, 6 picots).

Rnd 2: Ch 1, sc in first st, ch 6, skip next st and next picot, (sc in next st, ch 6, skip next st and next picot) 5 times, join.

Rnd 3: Sl st in first ch sp, (ch 1, sc, hdc, 3 dc, ch 3, 3 dc, hdc, sc) in same sp, (sc, hdc, 3 dc, ch 3, 3 dc, hdc, sc) in each ch sp around, join, fasten off.

SECOND MOTIF

Rnds 1-2: Repeat same rnds of First Motif.

Rnd 3: Sl st in first ch sp, (ch 1, sc, hdc, 3 dc) in same sp, ch 1, sl st in any ch sp on rnd 3 of First Motif, ch 2, (3 dc, hdc, sc) in same sp as last dc on this Motif, (sc, hdc, 3 dc, ch 3, 3 dc, hdc, sc) in each ch sp around, join, fasten off.

THIRD MOTIF

Rnds 1-2: Repeat same rnds of First Motif.

Rnd 3: Sl st in first ch sp, (ch 1, sc, hdc, 3 dc) in same sp, ch 1, sl st in next ch sp of First Motif (see Joining Diagram), ch 2, (3 dc, hdc, sc) in same sp as last dc on this Motif, (sc, hdc, 3 dc) in next ch sp, ch 1, sl st in corresponding ch sp of last Motif (see Joining Diagram), ch 2, (3 dc, hdc, sc) in same sp as last dc on this Motif, (sc, hdc, 3 dc, ch 3, 3 dc, hdc, sc) in each ch sp around, join, fasten off.

For **forth, fifth and sixth Motifs,** repeat Third Motif 3 more times.

SEVENTH MOTIF

Rnds 1-2: Repeat same rnds of First Motif.

JOINING DIAGRAM
Join white here for Rnd 1 of Border.

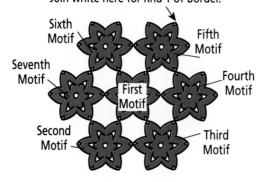

Sixth Motif

Fifth Motif

Seventh Motif

Fourth Motif

First Motif

Second Motif

Third Motif

Rnd 3: Sl st in first ch sp, (ch 1, sc, hdc, 3 dc) in same sp, ch 1, sl st in corresponding ch sp of Second Motif (see Joining Diagram), ch 2, (3 dc, hdc, sc) in same sp as last dc on this Motif, (sc, hdc, 3 dc) in next ch sp, ch 1, sl st in corresponding ch sp of First Motif (see Diagram), ch 2, (3 dc, hdc, sc) in same sp as last dc on this Motif, (sc, hdc, 3 dc) in next ch sp, ch 1, sl st in corresponding ch sp of last Motif (see Diagram), ch 2, (3 dc, hdc, sc) in same sp as last dc on this Motif, (sc, hdc, 3 dc, ch 3, 3 dc, hdc, sc) in each ch sp around, join, fasten off.

BORDER

Rnd 1: Working in unjoined ch sps around outer edge of Motifs, join white with sc in upper right ch sp as indicated on Diagram, (*ch 10, dc in next ch sp, ch 13, dc in first ch sp on next Motif, ch 10*, sc in next ch sp) 5 times; repeat between **, join with sl st in first sc.

Rnd 2: Ch 7, sl st in 4th ch from hook, *[(5 dc, picot, 5 dc, picot, 3 dc) in next ch sp, ch 3, skip next dc and next 6 chs, (dc, ch 5, dc) in next ch, ch 3, skip next 6 chs and next dc, (3 dc, picot, 5 dc, picot, 5 dc) in next ch sp], (dc, picot) in next sc; repeat from * 4 more times; repeat between [ ], join with sl st in 3rd ch of ch-7.

Rnd 3: Sl st in each of next 2 chs on first picot, ch 1, sc in same picot, (ch 7, sc in next picot) 2 times, *[ch 3, skip next ch-3 sp, dc in next ch-5 sp, (ch 2, dc in same ch sp) 4 times, ch 3, skip next ch-3 sp, sc in next picot], (ch 7, sc in next picot) 4 times; repeat from * 4 more times; repeat between [ ], ch 7, sc in next picot; to **join,** ch 3, tr in first sc.

Rnd 4: Ch 1, sc around joining tr, (ch 7, sc in next ch sp) 2 times, *[ch 3, skip next ch-3 sp, dc in next dc, (ch 1, dc in next ch sp, ch 1, dc in next dc) 4 times, ch 3, skip next ch-3 sp, sc in next ch sp], (ch 7, sc in next ch sp) 3 times; repeat from * 4 more times; repeat between [ ], join as before.

Rnd 5: Ch 1, sc around joining tr, *[(ch 7, sc in next ch sp) 2 times, ch 5, skip next ch-3 sp, dc in next dc, (ch 3, sc in next dc, picot, ch 3, dc in next dc) 4 times, ch 5, skip next ch-3 sp], sc in next ch sp; repeat from * 4 more times; repeat between [ ], join with sl st in first sc.

NOTE: For **V-st,** (dc, ch 3, dc) in next st or ch sp.

Rnd 6: Sl st in each of next 3 chs, ch 1, sc in same ch sp, *[ch 7, sc in next ch sp, ch 6, skip next ch-5 sp, V-st in next dc, (ch 3, skip next picot, V-st in next dc) 4 times, ch 6, skip next ch-5 sp], sc in next ch sp; repeat from * 4 more times; repeat between [ ], join.

Rnd 7: Sl st in each of next 3 chs, ch 1, sc in same ch sp, *[ch 9, skip next ch-6 sp, V-st in ch sp of next V-st, (V-st in next ch-3 sp, V-st in ch sp of next V-st) 4 times, ch 9, skip next ch-6 sp], sc in next ch sp; repeat from * 4 more times; repeat between [ ], join.

Rnd 8: Ch 6, dc in same st, *[skip next 3 chs, V-st in next ch, skip next 2 chs, V-st in next ch, V-st in each of next 9 V-sts, (skip next 2 chs, V-st in next ch) 2 times, skip next 3 chs], V-st in next sc; repeat from * 4 more times; repeat between [ ], join with sl st in 3rd ch of ch-6, fasten off.

Rnd 9: Join red with sc in any ch sp, (hdc, 2 dc) in same sp, *[tr in next dc, picot, tr in next dc, (2 dc, hdc, sc) in next ch sp, sc in next dc, picot, sc in next dc], (sc, hdc, 2 dc) in next ch sp; repeat from * 40 more times; repeat between [ ], join with sl st in first sc, fasten off.❊

Welcome Accents Instructions on page 32

Border Mitering Placement

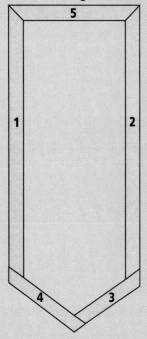

Bell Pull Stitch Count:
40 wide x 138 high

Approximate Design Size:
11-count 3⅝" x 12⅝"
14-count 2⅞" x 9⅞"
16-count 2½" x 8⅝"
18-count 2¼" x 7¾"
22-count 1⅞" x 6⅜"
28-count over two threads 2⅞" x 9⅞"

Alphabet & Numbers

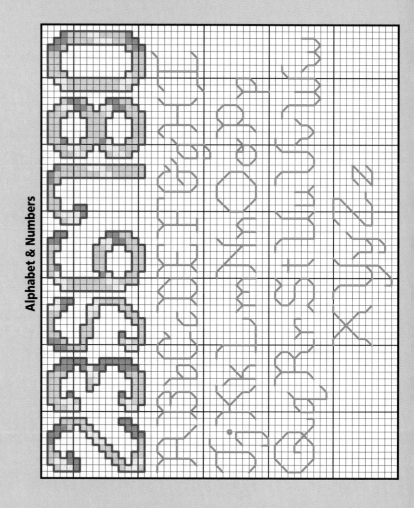

Welcome Accents

X	B'st	¼x	Fr	DMC	ANCHOR	J.&P. COATS	COLORS
				#221	#897	#3243	Darkest Victorian Rose
				#224	#893	#3239	Victorian Rose Lt.
				#319	#218	#6246	Spruce
				#320	#215	#6017	Pistachio Green Med.
				#725	#305	#2294	Topaz Med.
				#727	#293	#2289	Topaz Lt.
				#782	#308	#5308	Russet
				#801	#359	#5472	Coffee Brown Dk.
				#902	#897	#3083	Darkest Garnet
				#3371	#382	#5382	Darkest Brown
				#3722	#1027	#3241	Shell Pink Med.

Bell Pull

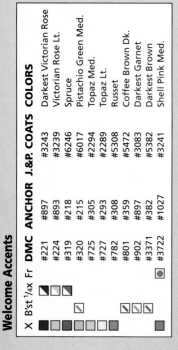

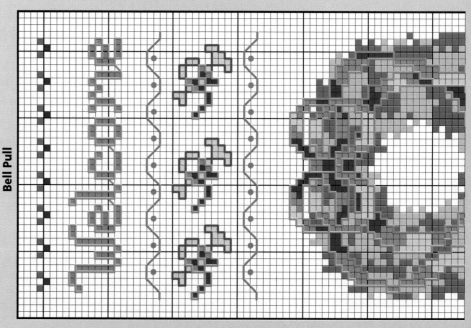

42

Angelic Silhouette Continued from page 36

Rows 15-20: Repeat rows 7-12 of first wing, beginning with 6 dc and 5 ch sps and ending with 21 sc.

Row 21: Ch 7, skip next 3 sts, dc in next st, (ch 4, skip next 3 sts, dc in next st) across, turn.

Row 22: Ch 1, sc in each st and 4 sc in each ch sp across to ch-7, 4 sc in ch-7 sp, sc in 3rd ch of ch-7, turn (26 sc).

Row 23: Ch 8, skip next 4 sts, dc in next st, (ch 5, skip next 4 sts, dc in next st) across, turn.

Row 24: Ch 1, sc in each st and 5 sc in each ch sp across to ch-8, 5 sc in ch-8 sp, sc in 3rd ch of ch-8, turn (31 sc).

Row 25: Ch 9, skip next 5 sts, dc in next st, (ch 6, skip next 5 sts, dc in next st) across, turn.

Row 26: Ch 1, sc in each st and 6 sc in each ch sp across to ch-9, 6 sc in ch-9 sp, sc in 3rd ch of ch-9, turn, fasten off (36 sc).

Row 27: Join with sc in end of row 6 at top of left-hand wing, sc in same row; working in ends of rows, *(2 sc in next row, sc in next row) 3 times, sc in next st, (ch 3, skip next st, sc in next st) 8 times, (sc in next row, 2 sc in next row) 3 times, 2 sc in next row*, 2 sc in next row on body, (2 sc in next row, sc in next row) 6 times, (ch 3, skip next st, sc in next st) 18 times, (sc in next row, 2 sc in next row) 6 times, 2 sc in next row, 2 sc in next row on wing; repeat between **, fasten off.

Edging

Row 1: Ch 116 or in multiples of 2 for desired length, dc in 6th ch from hook, (ch 1, skip next ch, dc in next ch) across, **do not** turn.

Rnd 2: Ch 1, 5 sc in end of row; working on opposite side of starting ch, sc in first ch, (sc in next ch sp, sc in ch at base of next st) across to ch-5 sp, 7 sc in ch-5 sp, sc in next st, (sc in next ch sp, sc in next st) across, join with sl st in first sc, fasten off.

Sew Edging to towel 3" from one short end; sew Angel centered 1½" above Edging.❂

Company's Coming Continued from page 37

ring, ch 5, skip next ch, (dc in next ch, ch 2, skip next ch) around, join with sl st in 3rd ch of ch-5 (25 dc, 25 ch sps).

Rnd 2: Ch 1, 3 sc in each ch sp around, join with sl st in first sc (75 sc).

Rnd 3: Ch 1, sc in first st, ch 5, skip next 2 sts, (sc in next st, ch 5, skip next 2 sts) around, join (25 ch sps).

Rnd 4: Ch 1, (3 sc, ch 3, 3 sc) in each ch sp around, join.

Rnd 5: Sl st in each of next 3 sts, (sl st, ch 1, sc) in next ch sp, ch 7, (sc in next ch sp, ch 7) around, join.

Rnd 6: Ch 1, (4 sc, ch 3, 4 sc) in each ch sp around, join, fasten off.

Weave ribbon through ch sps on rnd 1; tie ends into a bow.

EDGING

Row 1: Ch 4, (2 dc, ch 2, 3 dc) in 4th ch from hook, turn.

Rows 2-5: Ch 3, (3 dc, ch 2, 3 dc) in next ch-2 sp, turn. At end of last row, **do not** turn.

Row 6: Working in ch-3 sps at end of rows, (ch 5, sc in next ch-3 sp) 2 times, turn.

Row 7: Sl st in first ch-5 sp, ch 1, 9 sc in same ch sp, skip next sc, 5 sc in next ch-5 sp, turn.

Row 8: Ch 5, skip next 9 sts, sc in next st, turn.

Row 9: Sl st in first ch-5 sp, ch 1, (4 sc, ch 3, 4 sc) in same sp, 4 sc in next worked ch-5 sp, **do not** turn.

Rows 10-82: Repeat rows 2-9 consecutively, ending with row 2. At end of last row, fasten off.

Sew Edging to towel 2½" from one short end; sew Snowflake or Wreath centered 2" above Edging.❂

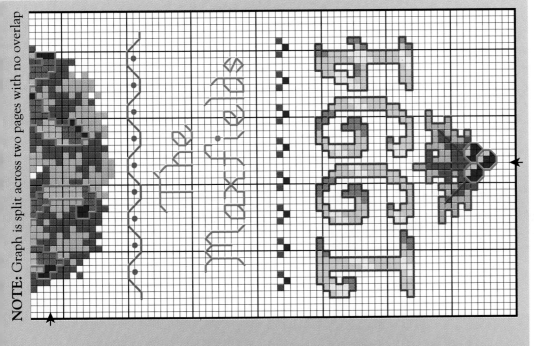

NOTE: Graph is split across two pages with no overlap

Hark! the Herald Angels Sing

The eternal symbol of peace and joy, angels are the crowning glory of your Christmas decorating theme. This heavenly assemblage of spirited messengers brings an inviting sense of well-being to all, and an unforgettable magic to each room graced by their presence. Opulently hued in gleaming white, gold and sky blue, these celestial beauties will be cherished by your family for many years to come.

Spirit of the Season

Designed by Jo Ann Maxwell

TECHNIQUE:
- Crochet

SIZE:
- 13" tall

MATERIALS:
- Size 10 bedspread cotton — 400 yds. white
- 50 yds. ecru
- 1 yd. iridescent ³⁄₁₆" ribbon
- 28 white 8-mm pearl beads
- 8-mm round acrylic stone
- Iridescent glitter
- 2" and 3" Styrofoam® balls
- 2" Styrofoam® egg
- 6"-tall Styrofoam® cone
- Automotive-type funnel
- Deep bowl measuring approximately 11" across top
- Rust-proof pins
- Liquid fabric stiffener
- Plastic wrap
- 4" x 8" piece of cardboard
- Craft glue or hot glue gun
- Tapestry needle
- No. 5 steel crochet hook or size needed to obtain gauge

GAUGE:
- 8 dc = 1"
- 3 dc rows = 1"

ANGEL

Rnd 1: Starting at top of head, with white, ch 6, sl st in first ch to form ring, ch 3, 29 dc in ring, join with sl st in top of ch-3 (30 dc).

Rnd 2: Ch 3, dc in next st, 2 dc in next st, (dc in each of next 2 sts, 2 dc in next st) around, join (40).

Rnds 3-13: Ch 2, hdc in each st around, join with sl st in top of ch-2. At end of last rnd, insert 2" foam ball.

Rnd 14: Ch 2, skip next st, (hdc in next st, skip next st) around, join (20).

Rnd 15: Ch 3, dc in same st, 2 dc in each st around, join with sl st in top of ch-3 (40).

Rnds 16-21: Ch 3, dc in each st around, join.

Rnd 22: Ch 1, sc in first st, (ch 5, sc in next st) around; to **join,** ch 2, dc in first sc (40 ch sps).

Rnds 23-29: Ch 1, sc around joining dc, (ch 5, sc in next ch sp) around, join as before.

Rnds 30-37: Ch 1, sc around joining st, (ch 6, sc in next ch sp) around; to **join,** ch 2, tr in first sc.

Rnds 38-42: Ch 1, sc around joining tr, (ch 7, sc in next ch sp) around; to **join,** ch 3, tr in first sc.

Rnd 43: Ch 1, sc around joining tr, ch 7, (sc in next ch sp, ch 7) around, join with sl st in first sc.

NOTE: For **triple picot (tr picot),** ch 3, sl st in 2nd ch from hook, sl st in next ch, sl st in center ch of ch-7 again, ch 4, sl st in 2nd ch from hook, sl st in each of next 2 chs, sl st in center ch of ch-7 again, ch 3, sl st in 2nd ch from hook, sl st in next ch, sl st in center ch of ch-7 again.

Rnd 44: Sl st in next ch, ch 5, dc in next ch, (ch 2, dc in next ch) 5 times, sl st in center ch of next ch-7, tr picot, *dc in first ch of next ch-7, (ch 2, dc in next ch) 6 times, sl st in center ch of next ch-7, tr picot; repeat from * around, join with sl st in 3rd ch of ch-5, fasten off.

RIGHT WING

Row 1: With white, ch 5, sl st in first ch to form ring, ch 3, 10 dc in ring, turn (11 dc).

Row 2: Ch 4, 4 tr in same st, dc in each of 9 sts, 5 tr in last st, turn (19 sts).

Row 3: Ch 8, sc in next st, (ch 5, sc in next st) 4 times, sc in next 6 sts, (ch 5, sc in next st) 6 times, ch 5, dc in last st, turn.

Row 4: Ch 8, sc in first ch sp, (ch 5, sc in next ch sp) 6 times, ch 2, skip next 3 sts, sc in next st, ch 2, sc in next ch sp, (ch 5, sc in next ch sp) 4 times, ch 5, dc in 3rd ch of ch-8, turn.

Row 5: Ch 9, sc in first ch sp, (ch 6, sc in next ch sp) 4 times, ch 3, skip next ch-2 sp, sc in next sc, ch 3, skip next ch-2 sp, sc in next ch sp, (ch 6, sc in next ch sp) 6 times, ch 6, dc in 3rd ch of ch-8, turn.

Row 6: Ch 9, sc in first ch sp, (ch 6, sc in next ch sp) 6 times, ch 4, skip next ch-3 sp, sc in next sc, ch 4, skip next ch-3 sp, sc in next ch sp, (ch 6, sc in next ch sp) 4 times, ch 6, dc in 3rd ch of ch-9, turn.

Row 7: Ch 10, sc in first ch sp, (ch 7, sc in next ch sp) 4 times, ch 5, skip next ch-4 sp, sc in next sc, ch 5, skip next ch-4 sp, sc in next ch sp, (ch 7, sc in next ch sp) 6 times, ch 7, sc in 3rd ch of ch-9, turn.

Row 8: Ch 10, sc in first ch sp, (ch 7, sc in next ch sp) 6 times, ch 6, skip next ch-5 sp, sc in next sc, ch 6, skip next ch-5 sp, sc in next ch sp, (ch 7, sc in next ch sp) 4 times, ch 7, dc in 3rd ch of ch-10, turn.

Row 9: Ch 10, sc in first ch sp, (ch 7, sc in next ch sp) 5 times, ch 3, sc in next sc, ch 3, sc in next ch sp, (ch 7, sc in next ch sp) 7 times, ch 7, dc in 3rd ch of ch-10, turn.

Row 10: Ch 5, dc in 2nd ch of next ch-7, (ch 2, dc in next ch) 5 times, *sl st in center ch of next ch-7, triple picot, dc in first ch of next ch-7, (ch 2, dc in next ch) 6 times*; repeat between ** 2 more times, sc in next ch sp, ch 7, skip next ch-3 sp, sc in next sc, ch 7, skip next ch-3 sp, sc in next ch sp, dc in first ch of next ch-7, (ch 2, dc in next ch) 6 times; repeat between ** 2 more times, fasten off.

LEFT WING

Row 1: Repeat same row of Right Wing.

Row 2: Ch 1, sc in each st across, turn.

Rows 3-11: Repeat rows 2-10 of Right Wing.

ARM (make 2)

With white, ch 22, 5 dc in 4th ch from hook, dc in next 8 chs; for **elbow,** 5 dc in next ch; dc in next 8 chs; for **hand,** (5 dc, ch 3, sl st) in last ch, fasten off.

Continued on page 57

Guardian Angels

Designed by Vicki Blizzard

CUTTING INSTRUCTIONS

NOTE: Graphs on page 56.

A: For bodies, cut eight according to graph.

B: For arms, cut eight according to graph.

C: For wings, cut eight according to graph.

D: For halos, cut four according to graph.

E: For hearts, cut ten according to graph.

F: For cloud tops and bottoms, cut two each according to graphs.

STITCHING INSTRUCTIONS

1: Using colors indicated and Continental Stitch, work A, B, C (four of each B and C on opposite side of canvas), E and F pieces according to graphs; fill in uncoded areas using white and Continental Stitch. With pearl/white cord for halos and with matching colors, Overcast unfinished edges of B-E pieces.

2: Using colors indicated and Straight Stitch, embroider facial detail on four A pieces as indicated on graph.

3: For each body, holding one of each A wrong sides together, with matching colors, Whipstitch together, stuffing with fiberfill before closing.

4: For top and bottom clouds, holding matching F pieces wrong sides together, with matching colors, Whipstitch together, stuffing with fiberfill before closing.

5: Glue two wings to back and two beads for eyes to face of each angel.

NOTES: Cut eight 9" lengths of white and four 9" lengths of lt. blue ⅛" ribbon; tie into bows. Trim streamers short on four white bows.

6: Glue one small bow to back of each angel between wings. Glue one of each color bow and one ribbon rose to neckline of each angel; shape and glue streamers to front of body as shown in photo. Glue hair, halos and arms to angels as shown.

7: Slide top and bottom clouds together at slots; with sail blue, sew plastic ring to center top. Glue glitter to clouds and angels as desired or as shown. Thread remaining ribbons through center bottom of clouds; glue hearts to ribbon and trim ends of streamers as desired.❋

TECHNIQUE:
• Plastic Canvas

SIZE:
• 14" across x about 21" long

MATERIALS:
• Four sheets of 7-count plastic canvas
• 6 yds. white and 4 yds. lt. blue ⅛" satin ribbon
• 4 yds. white and 3 yds. lt. blue ¼" satin ribbon
• White curly doll hair
• Glow-in-the-dark glitter
• Four white ¼" satin ribbon roses
• One white ⅝" plastic ring
• Eight black 4-mm half-round beads
• Polyester fiberfill
• Monofilament fishing line
• Craft glue or glue gun
• #3 pearl cotton or six-strand embroidery floss (for amount see Color Key on page 56)
• Pearlized cord (for amount see Color Key)
• Worsted-weight or plastic canvas yarn (for amounts see Color Key)

Celestial Beauty

Designed by Teresa S. Hannaway

TECHNIQUE:
• Plastic Canvas

SIZE:
• About 10" tall

MATERIALS:
• 1½ sheets of 7-count plastic canvas
• One 6" plastic canvas circle
• 2 yds. gold metallic ¼" rickrack
• White curly doll hair
• One 18" length of 20-gauge floral wire
• Craft glue or glue gun
• Metallic cord (for amount see Color Key)
• Pearlized cord (for amounts see Color Key)
• Worsted-weight or plastic canvas yarn (for amounts see Color Key)

CUTTING INSTRUCTIONS

A: For head, cut one according to graph on page 57.

B: For dress pieces, cut six according to graph.

C: For sleeves, cut two according to graph.

D: For arms, cut four according to graph.

E: For wings, cut four according to graph.

F: For base, cut away center of circle, leaving only outer two rows of holes (no graph).

STITCHING INSTRUCTIONS

NOTE: F piece is unworked.

1: Using colors and stitches indicated, work A (overlap three holes at ends as indicated on graph and work through both thicknesses at overlap area to join), B (leave indicated area on two pieces unworked for sleeve attachment), C, D and E (two of each arm and wing on opposite side of canvas) pieces according to graphs.

2: Using pearl/blue and Cross Stitch for eyes, white yarn and French Knot for nose and pearl/white and Straight Stitch for wings, embroider detail on A and E pieces as indicated.

3: With white yarn, Whipstitch X edges of A together as indicated. For each sleeve, folding edges of one C wrong sides together, Whipstitch together between arrows as indicated; Whipstitch one sleeve to unworked area of each dress piece as indicated.

4: With sleeves on opposite sides of dress (see photo), with matching colors, Whipstitch B pieces together; Overcast unfinished

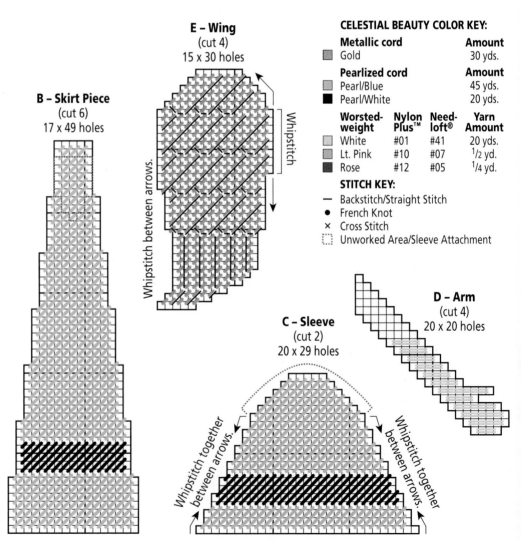

E – Wing
(cut 4)
15 x 30 holes

Whipstitch between arrows.

Whipstitch

B – Skirt Piece
(cut 6)
17 x 49 holes

C – Sleeve
(cut 2)
20 x 29 holes

Whipstitch together between arrows.

Whipstitch together between arrows.

D – Arm
(cut 4)
20 x 20 holes

CELESTIAL BEAUTY COLOR KEY:

	Metallic cord	Amount
▦	Gold	30 yds.

	Pearlized cord	Amount
▦	Pearl/Blue	45 yds.
■	Pearl/White	20 yds.

	Worsted-weight	Nylon Plus™	Needloft®	Yarn Amount
▦	White	#01	#41	20 yds.
▦	Lt. Pink	#10	#07	½ yd.
▦	Rose	#12	#05	¼ yd.

STITCH KEY:
- — Backstitch/Straight Stitch
- • French Knot
- × Cross Stitch
- ⬚ Unworked Area/Sleeve Attachment

edges of sleeves. With white yarn, Whipstitch head and dress together; with pearl/blue, Whipstitch F to bottom edges of dress.

5: For each arm, holding two D pieces wrong sides together, with white yarn, Whipstitch together. For each wing, holding two E pieces wrong sides together, with pearl/white, Whipstitch together between arrows as indicated; to join wings, Whipstitch unfinished edges together as indicated.

6: Glue wings to back of dress, arms inside sleeves and rickrack trim to dress as shown in photo; glue hair to head as desired. For halo, form a circle about 2" across with floral wire; leave a stem about 1" long (see Halo Assembly Diagram on page 56). Cut off excess wire. Glue rickrack wrong sides together around wire circle (see photo). Push halo stem into head and glue to secure. Tie remaining rickrack into a bow and glue to front of dress as shown.❈

Seraphs & Stars

Designed by Mary K. Perry

CUTTING INSTRUCTIONS

A: For Large 7-count Angel, cut two from 7-count according to graph.

B: For Small 7-count Angel, cut two from 7-count according to graph.

C: For 10-count Angel, cut two from 10-count according to graph.

D: For 7-count Star, cut two from 7-count according to graph.

E: For 10-count Star, cut two from 10-count according to graph.

NOTE: For candle ring, cut six C pieces; Whipstitch finished pieces together at hem of skirts as shown in photo.

STITCHING INSTRUCTIONS

NOTE: Separate 1 yd. of maple into 2-ply or nylon plastic canvas yarn into 1-ply strands; use 2-ply (or 1-ply) maple for hair on C.

1: Using colors and stitches indicated, work A-C (one each on opposite side of canvas) pieces according to graphs; with matching colors, Overcast unfinished edges as indicated on graphs. Holding matching pieces wrong sides together, Whipstitch unfinished edges together.

2: Using colors indicated and Backstitch, embroider gown detail as indicated.

3: Using colors and stitches indicated, work D and E pieces according to graphs. Holding matching pieces wrong sides together, Whipstitch together as indicated; Overcast unfinished edges.

4: For plant pokes, glue one stick inside each Angel or Star. For ornaments, hang as desired. ✶

SERAPHS & STARS COLOR KEY:

Heavy metallic braid, ribbon or cord		Amount
▨	Pearl/White	17 yds.
■	Gold	8 yds.
Medium metallic braid		**Amount**
■	Gold	19 yds.
3-ply yarn		**Amount**
■	White	12 yds.

Worsted-weight	Nylon Plus™	Need-loft®	Yarn Amount
White	#01	#41	15 yds.
Maple	#35	#13	4 yds.
Peach	#46	#47	2 yds.

STITCH KEY:
— Backstitch/Straight Stitch

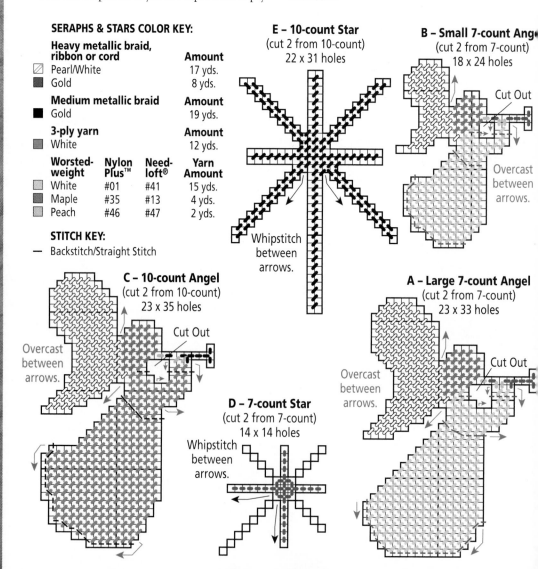

E – 10-count Star
(cut 2 from 10-count)
22 x 31 holes
Whipstitch between arrows.

B – Small 7-count Angel
(cut 2 from 7-count)
18 x 24 holes
Cut Out
Overcast between arrows.

C – 10-count Angel
(cut 2 from 10-count)
23 x 35 holes
Cut Out
Overcast between arrows.

D – 7-count Star
(cut 2 from 7-count)
14 x 14 holes
Whipstitch between arrows.

A – Large 7-count Angel
(cut 2 from 7-count)
23 x 33 holes
Cut Out
Overcast between arrows.

Radiant Messenger

Designed by Jocelyn Sass

CUTTING INSTRUCTIONS

A: For body, cut two according to graph.
B: For head, cut one according to graph.
C: For arms, cut two according to graph.

STITCHING INSTRUCTIONS

NOTE: One A is unworked for back.

1: Using colors and stitches indicated, work one A for front, B and C (one on opposite side of canvas) pieces according to graphs; with matching colors, Overcast unfinished edges of B and C pieces. Holding unworked A to wrong side of worked piece, Whipstitch together.

NOTE: Cut ribbon in half; holding ribbons together, tie into a bow.

2: Glue head, arms, bow, excelsior, baby's breath and ribbon roses to Angel as shown in photo. Glue sawtooth hanger to back.❈

TECHNIQUE:
• Plastic Canvas

SIZE:
• 8" x 14"

MATERIALS:
• Two sheets of 12" x 18" or larger 7-count plastic canvas
• 1⅓ yds. dk. teal ¼" satin picot-edged ribbon
• Nine dk. teal ½" ribbon roses
• 2" sawtooth hanger
• Wood excelsior
• Small bunch of baby's breath
• Pearlized cord (for amount see Color Key)
• Worsted-weight or plastic canvas yarn (for amount see Color Key)

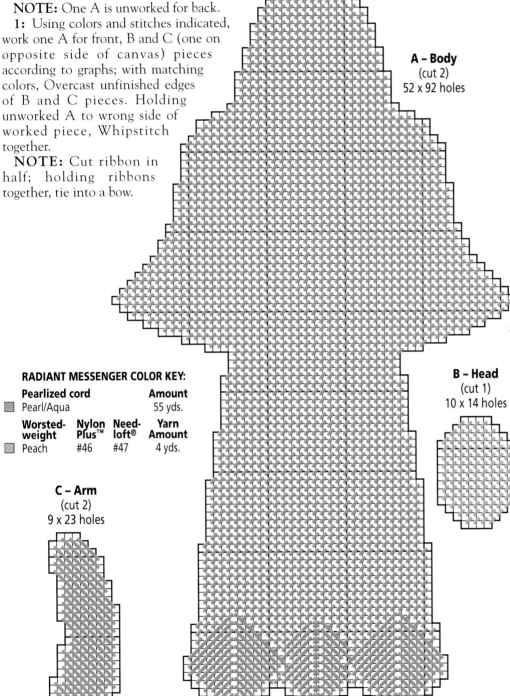

A – Body
(cut 2)
52 x 92 holes

B – Head
(cut 1)
10 x 14 holes

C – Arm
(cut 2)
9 x 23 holes

RADIANT MESSENGER COLOR KEY:

Pearlized cord			Amount
▢ Pearl/Aqua			55 yds.

Worsted-weight	Nylon Plus™	Need-loft®	Yarn Amount
▢ Peach	#46	#47	4 yds.

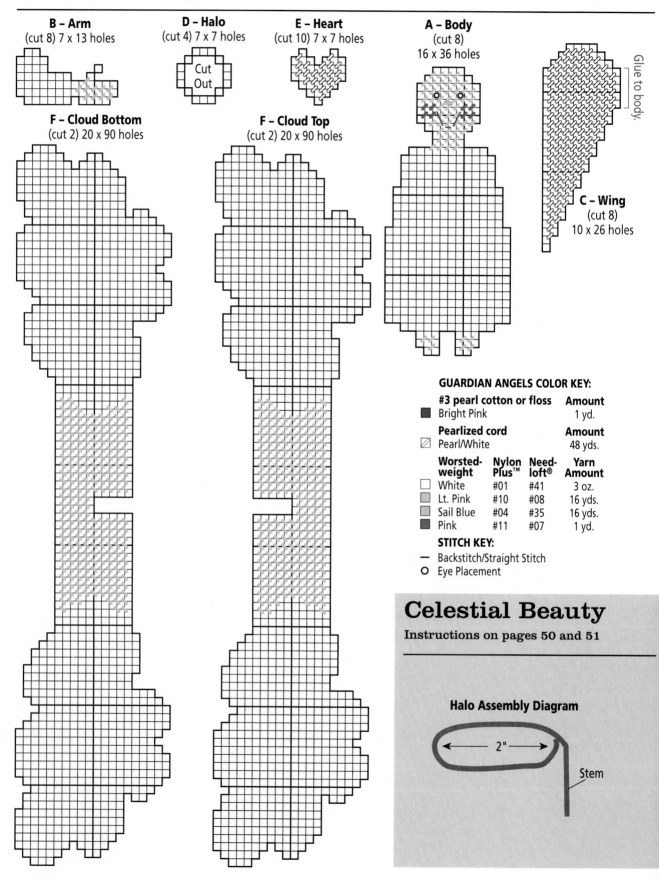

B – Arm
(cut 8) 7 x 13 holes

D – Halo
(cut 4) 7 x 7 holes

Cut
Out

E – Heart
(cut 10) 7 x 7 holes

A – Body
(cut 8)
16 x 36 holes

Glue to body.

C – Wing
(cut 8)
10 x 26 holes

F – Cloud Bottom
(cut 2) 20 x 90 holes

F – Cloud Top
(cut 2) 20 x 90 holes

GUARDIAN ANGELS COLOR KEY:

#3 pearl cotton or floss			Amount
■ Bright Pink			1 yd.
Pearlized cord			**Amount**
◫ Pearl/White			48 yds.

Worsted-weight	Nylon Plus™	Need-loft®	Yarn Amount
□ White	#01	#41	3 oz.
▨ Lt. Pink	#10	#08	16 yds.
▨ Sail Blue	#04	#35	16 yds.
■ Pink	#11	#07	1 yd.

STITCH KEY:
— Backstitch/Straight Stitch
O Eye Placement

Celestial Beauty

Instructions on pages 50 and 51

Halo Assembly Diagram

← 2" →

Stem

Spirit of the Season Continued from page 46

SNOWFLAKE (make 9)

Rnd 1: With white, ch 4, sl st in first ch to form ring, (ch 11, sl st in ring) 12 times (12 ch sps).

Rnd 2: Sl st in next 6 chs, ch 1, sc in same ch sp, ch 7, (sc in next ch sp, ch 7) around, join with sl st in first sc.

Rnd 3: Sl st in first ch of next ch-7, ch 5, dc in next ch, (ch 2, dc in next ch) 5 times, sl st in center ch of next ch-7, triple picot, *dc in first ch of next ch-7, (ch 2, dc in next ch) 6 times, sl st in center ch of next ch-7, triple picot; repeat from * around, join with sl st 3rd ch of ch-5, fasten off.

HALO

With white, ch 34, sl st in first ch to form ring, ch 2, 2 hdc in next ch, (hdc in next ch, 2 hdc in next ch) around, join with sl st in top of ch-2, fasten off.

FINISHING

1: Cover foam egg with plastic wrap; insert large end first into Body below Head, forming bodice. Tie a strand of white between head and bodice, forming neck; pull tight and secure.

2: Cut narrow end off funnel. For form, turn bowl upside down, place cone on top of bowl and place funnel on top of cone. Place Angel over form to check fit and trim top of cone if needed; cover with plastic wrap.

3: Apply fabric stiffener to Angel according to manufacturer's instructions, place over form; shape as shown in photo, stuffing waist area with plastic wrap if desired. Let dry completely before removing forms. Glue 6" of iridescent ribbon around waist.

4: Stiffen seven Snowflakes, cupping them slightly as they dry. Glue one bead to center of each; glue glitter around the bead and to each triple picot. Glue Snowflakes around Angel's skirt as shown.

5: Stiffen each Arm; glue to each side of bodice.

6: Wrap 3" ball with plastic wrap. Apply stiffener to remaining Snowflakes and shape over ball. Let dry. For each sleeve, glue edges of Snowflake together according to Sleeve Diagram; glue glitter to each triple picot. Glue sleeves to each side of Angel over top of Arms.

7: Stiffen Wings, shaping as shown. Glue glitter to triple picots; glue wings to back of bodice as shown.

8: Stiffen Halo; glue 15 beads around top and glitter around edge.

9: For hair, wrap ecru around narrow width of cardboard 250 times, being careful to keep wraps flat. Cut wraps at one edge, forming 8" strands. Glue strands to top of head, letting hair fall over back of head.

10: For sides, wrap ecru around wide width of cardboard 100 times. Cut wraps at one edge, forming 16" strands. Glue center over top of head with ends falling to each side of head

11: For part, with tapestry needle or or pin, spread a small amount of glue over center of a few strands and press to crease. Continue across entire top layer. Let dry. Trim ends even. Glue Halo to top of head.

12: For bouquet, glue remaining ribbon in a circle of loops leaving ends for streamers. Glue stone to center of circle and 6 beads around stone. Glue back of bouquet to hand. Curl streamers and glue to skirt.❁

Sleeve Folding Diagram

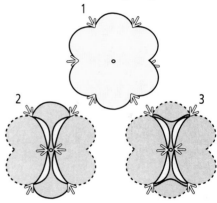

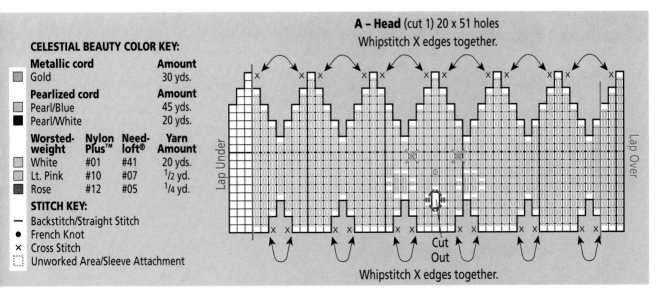

A – Head (cut 1) 20 x 51 holes
Whipstitch X edges together.

CELESTIAL BEAUTY COLOR KEY:

	Metallic cord	Amount
☐	Gold	30 yds.

	Pearlized cord	Amount
☐	Pearl/Blue	45 yds.
■	Pearl/White	20 yds.

	Worsted-weight	Nylon Plus™	Need-loft®	Yarn Amount
☐	White	#01	#41	20 yds.
☐	Lt. Pink	#10	#07	½ yd.
▨	Rose	#12	#05	¼ yd.

STITCH KEY:
- — Backstitch/Straight Stitch
- • French Knot
- × Cross Stitch
- ⬚ Unworked Area/Sleeve Attachment

Lap Under

Lap Over

Cut Out

Whipstitch X edges together.

Sweet Memories

Christmas just wouldn't be Christmas
without a lavish supply of
confectionary treats, so we put
together this tasteful collection of
mouth-watering designs sure to
satisfy even the sourest "Scrooge."
Highlighted by a gingerbread village
that includes a cookie canister,
napkin holder and coaster set,
this grouping is one indulgence that
won't add inches to your waistline.

Gingerbread Village

Designed by Celia Lange Designs

TECHNIQUE:
- Plastic Canvas

SIZE:
- Cookie Canister is 8" x 8" x 9¼" tall
- Doorstop is 3¼" x 8½" x 9¼" tall
- Each Coaster is 4¾" x 5¼"
- Coaster Holder is 1¾" x 5" x about 2" tall

MATERIALS:
- 12 sheets of 7-count plastic canvas
- Three sheets of 10-count plastic canvas
- Craft corkboard
- One white and two brown 9" x 12" sheets of felt
- Lightweight cardboard
- Four ¾" and five ½" red sew-on heart buttons
- 330 green and 90 topaz 4-mm. round faceted beads
- Beading needle and thread to match buttons and beads
- Zip-close bag filled with marbles or gravel (for Doorstop)
- Craft glue or glue gun
- #3 pearl cotton or six-strand embroidery floss (for amounts see individual Color Keys on pages 69 and 70; double amounts if using floss)
- #5 pearl cotton or six-strand embroidery floss (for amounts see Coasters & Holder Color Key)
- Worsted-weight or plastic canvas yarn (for amounts see Canister & Doorstop Color Key)

CANISTER
CUTTING INSTRUCTIONS
NOTES: Use 7-count canvas throughout. Graphs and diagrams on pages 68 and 69.

A: For front facade, cut one according to graph.

B: For chimney, cut one according to graph.

C: For door frame, cut one according to graph.

D: For roof snow, cut one according to graph.

E: For chimney snow, cut one according to graph.

F: For small shutters, cut two according to graph.

G: For large shutters, cut sixteen according to graph.

H: For front and lining, cut two (one for front and one for lining) 31 x 51 holes (no graphs).

I: For sides and linings, cut six (three for sides and three for linings) 31 x 51 holes (no lining graph).

J: For bottom and lining, cut two (one for bottom and one for lining) 51 x 51 holes (no graphs).

K: For corner braces, cut four according to graph.

L: For lid and lining, cut two (one for lid and one for lining) 52 x 52 holes (no graphs).

M: For lid handle top and lining, cut two 10 x 10 holes (no graph).

N: For lid handle base, cut five 4 x 4 holes (no graph).

O: For front facade linings, using A as a pattern, cut two (one from cardboard and one from brown felt) ⅛" smaller at all edges.

STITCHING INSTRUCTIONS
NOTE: N and lining H-J, L and M pieces are unworked.

Continued on page 68

Ribbon Candy Bow

Designed by Jocelyn Sass

TECHNIQUE:
• Plastic Canvas

SIZE:
• 1⅝" x 3⅝"

MATERIALS:
• ½ sheet of 7-count plastic canvas
• One 2¾" French barrette
• ⅛ yd. white ¼" satin ribbon
• Craft glue or glue gun
• Worsted-weight or plastic canvas yarn (for amounts see Color Key on page 71)

CUTTING INSTRUCTIONS
NOTE: Graphs on page 71.
A: For large bow, cut one according to graph.
B: For small bow, cut one according to graph.

STITCHING INSTRUCTIONS
1: Using colors and stitches indicated, work A and B pieces according to graphs. With matching colors, Overcast unfinished edges.
2: For each bow, holding ends of one bow wrong sides together, with white, Whipstitch together as indicated on graph.
3: Hold bows together as shown in photo and tie ribbon into a tight knot around centers to secure; trim ends of ribbon. Glue French barrette to back.❋

Remembrance Poinsettia

Designed by Kathleen J. Fischer

TECHNIQUE:
• Plastic Canvas

SIZE:
• 1" x 2¾" square

MATERIALS:
• ½ sheet of 10-count plastic canvas
• Craft glue or glue gun
• ⅟₁₆" metallic ribbon or heavy metallic braid (for amount see Color Key on page 71)
• Four-strand high luster embroidery thread (for amounts see Color Key)
• Six-strand embroidery floss (for amounts see Color Key)

CUTTING INSTRUCTIONS
NOTE: Graphs on page 71.
A: For box top and bottom, cut two (one for top and one for bottom) 27 x 27 holes.
B: For box sides, cut four 7 x 27 holes.
C: For poinsettia bracts, cut two according to graph.
D: For poinsettia center, cut one according to graph.

STITCHING INSTRUCTIONS
NOTES: Separate embroidery thread into 2-ply and floss into 3-ply strands.
To blend each color, hold one 2-ply strand of embroidery thread and one 3-ply strand of embroidery floss together.
1: Using blended colors and stitches indicated, work A-D pieces according to graphs. With red, Overcast unfinished edges of C and D pieces.
2: Using metallic ribbon or braid and French Knot, embroider detail as indicated on D graph.
3: Holding A and B pieces wrong sides together, with matching colors, Whipstitch together. Glue poinsettia bracts and center to box as shown in photo.❋

Candy Cane Collar

Designed by Jacquelyn Fox

STITCHING INSTRUCTIONS

1: Center and stitch design, stitching over two threads and using two strands floss for Cross Stitch and one strand floss for Backstitch. Trim seams and clip curves; press. Slip stitch collar and lining together.❆

Graph on page 67

TECHNIQUE:
- Cross Stitch & Sewing

MATERIALS:
- White Irish Linen Collar

Miss Christmas

Designed by Rosanne Kropp

TECHNIQUE:
• Crochet

SIZE:
• 8" tall

MATERIALS:
• Sport yarn — 6 oz. red, 3 oz. white
• White ¼" button
• 8" craft doll
• Two red 9-mm ribbon roses
• Eleven red 18-mm ribbon roses with leaves
• 1 yd. red. ⅜" ribbon
• 18" red ⅛" ribbon
• White sewing thread
• Craft glue or hot glue gun
• Sewing and tapestry needles
• F and G crochet hooks or sizes needed to obtain gauges

GAUGES:
• F hook, 9 sc sts = 2"; 9 sc rows = 2"
• G hook, 4 dc sts = 1"; 2 dc rows = 1"

DRESS

Row 1: For **bodice,** starting at neck edge, with E hook and white, ch 12, 2 sc in 2nd ch from hook, 2 sc in next ch, (sc in next ch, 2 sc in each of next 2 chs) 3 times, turn (19 sc).

Row 2: Ch 1, sc in first st, (2 sc in each of next 2 sts, sc in each of next 3 sts) 3 times, 2 sc in each of next 2 sts, sc in last st, turn (27).

Row 3: Ch 1, sc in each of first 2 sts, (2 sc in each of next 2 sts, sc in next 5 sts) 3 times, 2 sc in each of next 2 sts, sc in each of last 2 sts, turn (35).

Row 4: Ch 1, sc in each of first 3 sts, (2 sc in each of next 2 sts, sc in next 7 sts) 3 times, 2 sc in each of next 2 sts, sc in each of last 3 sts, turn (43).

Row 5: Ch 1, sc in each st across, turn.

Row 6: Ch 1, sc in first 5 sts; for **armhole,** skip next 11 sts; sc in next 11 sts; for **armhole,** skip next 11 sts; sc in last 5 sts, turn (21).

Rows 7-8: Ch 1, sc in each st across, turn.

Rnd 9: Working this rnd in **back lps** only, sl st in each st around, join with sl st in first sl st.

NOTES: For **shell,** (2 dc, ch 1, 2 dc) in next st.

For **V-st,** (dc, ch 1, dc) in next st.

Rnd 10: Working this rnd in **front lps** only, for **skirt,** ch 3, shell in first st, (dc in next st, shell in next st) around, join with sl st in top of ch-3 (11 shells, 11 dc).

Rnd 11: Ch 4, dc in first st, shell in ch sp of next shell, (V-st in next dc, shell in ch sp of next shell) around, join with sl st in 3rd ch of ch-4.

Rnd 12: (Sl st, ch 4, dc) in first ch sp, shell in next shell, (V-st in ch sp of next V-st, shell in next shell) around, join.

Rnd 13: (Sl st, ch 4, V-st) in first ch sp, shell in next shell, *(V-st, ch 1, dc) in next V-st, shell in next shell; repeat from * around, join.

Rnd 14: (Sl st, ch 4, dc) in first ch sp, ch 2, V-st in next V-st, shell in next shell, (V-st in next V-st, ch 2, V-st in next ch-1 sp, shell in next shell) around, join.

Rnd 15: (Sl st, ch 4, dc) in first ch sp, ch 3, V-st in next V-st, shell in next shell, (V-st in next V-st, ch 3, V-st in next V-st, shell in next shell) around, join.

Rnd 16: (Sl st, ch 4, dc) in first ch sp, ch 5, V-st in next V-st, shell in next shell, (V-st in next V-st, ch 5, V-st in next V-st, shell in next shell) around, join.

Rnd 17: (Sl st, ch 4, dc) in first ch sp, ch 6, V-st in next V-st, shell in next shell, (V-st in next V-st, ch 6, V-st in next V-st, shell in next shell) around, join.

Rnd 18: (Sl st, ch 1, sc) in first ch sp, *[ch 2, (sc, ch 3, sc) in next ch-6 sp, ch 2, sc in next V-st, ch 1, (dc, ch 1) 4 times in next shell], sc in next V-st; repeat from * 9 more times; repeat between [ ], join with sl st in first sc.

Rnd 19: Sl st in each of next 2 chs, *sl st in next st, 4 sc in next ch sp, sl st in next st, ch 2, skip next ch sp, dc in next ch-1 sp, (dc, ch 3, dc) in each of next 3 ch-1 sps, dc in next ch-1 sp, ch 2, skip next ch sp; repeat from * around, join, fasten off.

SLEEVES

Row 1: With wrong side facing you, working in 11 skipped sts on one armhole, with E hook and white, join with sc in first st, sc in next 10 sts, turn (11 sc).

Rows 2-4: Ch 1, sc in each st across, turn. At end of last row, fasten off.

Sew Sleeve seam.

For **ruffle,** join white with sc in seam, (ch 3, sc, ch 3) in same seam, (sc, ch 3, sc, ch 3) in each st around, join with sl st in first sc, fasten off.

Repeat on other armhole.

COLLAR

Row 1: With wrong side facing you, working in starting ch on opposite side of row 1 on Bodice, with E hook and white, join with sl st in first ch, (ch 4, dc) in same ch, V-st in each ch across, turn (11 V-sts).

Row 2: (Sl st, ch 4, dc) in first ch sp, V-st in each V-st across, turn.

Row 3: (Sl st, ch 1, sc, ch 3, sc, ch 3, sc) in first ch sp, (sc, ch 3, sc, ch 3, sc, ch 3, sc) in each of next 9 V-sts, (sc, ch 3, sc, ch 3, sc) in last V-st, **do not** turn, fasten off.

Row 4: Join red with sl st in first sc, (ch 3, sl st in next sc) 2 times, sl st in next sc, *(ch 3, sl st in next sc) 3 times, sl st in next sc; repeat from * across to last 2 ch sps, (ch 3, sl st in next sc) 2 times, fasten off.

PLACKET

Row 1: With E hook and white, join with sc in end of row 1 on left Bodice; for **buttonhole,** ch 1, sc in same row; sc in each row across to opposite end of row 1 on right

Bodice, turn.

Row 2: Ch 1, sc in each st across, fasten off.

Sew button to Placket opposite buttonhole.

PETTICOAT

Rnd 1: Working in **back lps** of rnd 9, with G hook and red, join with sl st in first st, ch 3, dc in same st, (3 dc in next st, 2 dc in next st) around, join with sl st in top of ch-3 (52 dc).

Rnd 2: Ch 3, dc in each of next 2 sts, 2 dc in next st, (dc in each of next 3 sts, 2 dc in next st) around, join (65).

Rnd 3: Ch 3, dc in each of next 3 sts, 2 dc in next st, (dc in next 4 sts, 2 dc in next st) around, join (78).

Rnd 4: Ch 3, dc in next 4 sts, 2 dc in next st, (dc in next 5 sts, 2 dc in next st) around, join (91).

Rnd 5: Ch 3, dc in next 5 sts, 2 dc in next st, (dc in next 6 sts, 2 dc in next st) around, join (104).

Rnd 6: Ch 3, dc in next 6 sts, 2 dc in next st, (dc in next 7 sts, 2 dc in next st) around, join (117).

Rnd 7: Ch 3, dc in next 7 sts, 2 dc in next st, (dc in next 8 sts, 2 dc in next st) around, join (130).

Rnd 8: Ch 3, dc in next 8 sts, 2 dc in next st, (dc in next 9 sts, 2 dc in next st) around, join (143).

Rnd 9: Ch 3, dc in next 9 sts, 2 dc in next st, (dc in next 10 sts, 2 dc in next st) around, join (156).

Rnd 10: Ch 3, 4 dc in next st, (dc in next st, 4 dc in next st) around, join.

Rnd 11: Ch 3, dc in each st around, join, fasten off.

HAIR TRIM (make 2)

Rnd 1: With E hook and white, ch 2, 7 sc in 2nd ch from hook, join with sl st in first sc (7 sc).

Rnd 2: Ch 1, sc in first st, ch 4, (sc in next st, ch 4) around, join, fasten off.

FINISHING

1: Cut ⅛" ribbon in half. Tie each piece into a bow, trim ends. Glue one bow to center of each Hair Trim. Glue one 9-mm ribbon rose to each bow.

2: Run strand of white yarn through st at back of Hair Trim, tie around hair on one side of doll's head as shown in photo. Repeat with other Hair Trim on other side of doll's head.

3: Place Dress on doll. Tie ⅜" ribbon around waist.

4: Glue 18-mm ribbon roses evenly spaced around skirt at base of shells.✵

Bells & Bows

Designed by Celia Lange Designs

TECHNIQUE:
• Plastic Canvas

SIZE:
• 7½" x 13" and holds two 4½" x 5½" or slightly larger photos

MATERIALS:
• Two sheets of 7-count plastic canvas
• 1 yd. white ½" satin ribbon
• Six 25-mm. gold jingle bells
• Craft glue or glue gun
• Worsted-weight or plastic canvas yarn (for amounts see Color Key)

CUTTING INSTRUCTIONS

A: For fronts and backs, cut two for fronts according to graph and two for backs 41 x 49 holes.

B: For spine, cut two 3 x 49 holes.

STITCHING INSTRUCTIONS

1: Using colors and stitches indicated, work A and B pieces according to graphs.

2: Using green and Herringbone Overcast (see Stitch Illustration), Overcast unfinished cutout edges of front A pieces and one unfinished long edge of each front A as indicated on graph.

3: Using green and Herringbone Whipstitch (see Stitch Illustration), Whipstitch A and B pieces together according to Frame Assembly Diagram.

NOTE: Cut ribbon in half.

4: For each frame, tie one ribbon into a bow; glue bow and three bells to frame as desired or as shown in photo.✵

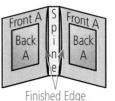

Frame Assembly Diagram

Step 1:
For spine, holding B pieces wrong sides together, Whipstitch short ends together.

Step 2:
Whipstitch spine and back A pieces together.

Step 3:
Holding A pieces wrong sides together, Whipstitch outside edges together.

Herringbone Overcast Stitch Illustration

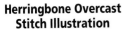

B – Spine
(cut 2)
3 x 49 holes

A – Front & Back (cut 2 each) 41 x 49 holes

Overcast between arrows.

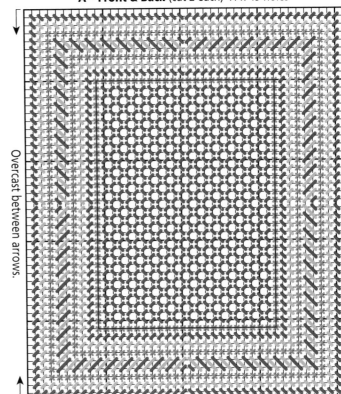

BELLS & BOWS COLOR KEY:

	Worsted-weight	Nylon Plus™	Need-loft®	Yarn Amount
■	Red	#19	#02	50 yds.
▨	Green	#58	#28	45 yds.
□	White	#01	#41	28 yds.

STITCH KEY:
□ Cut Out For Front Only

Herringbone Whipstitch Stitch Illustration

Candy Cane Collar Instructions on page 63

Stitch Count:
81 wide x 29 high

Approximate Design Size:
11-count 7⅜" x 2⅝"
14-count 5⅞" x 2⅛"
16-count 5⅛" x 1⅞"
18-count 4½" x 1⅝"
22-count 3¾" x 1⅜"
28-count over two threads 5⅞" x 2⅛"

Candy Cane Collar

X	B'st	DMC	ANCHOR	J.&P. COATS	COLORS
■		#304	#1006	#3410	Scarlet
▨		#415	#398	#8398	Silver
▨		#761	#1021	#3068	Salmon Lt.
▨		#813	#161	#7161	Sky Blue Med.
	◩	#814	#45	#3044	Garnet Very Dk.
■		#825	#162	#7181	Blue Dk.
	◩	#939	#152	#7160	Navy Blue Ultra Very Dk.
▨		#3712	#1023	#3071	Salmon Med.
□		#3756	#1037	#7975	Baby Blue Very Lt.
⊡		White	#2	#1001	White

Candy Cane Collar

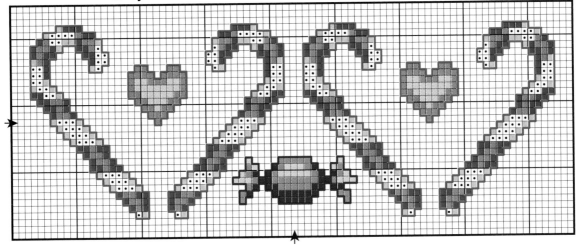

Gingerbread Village Continued from page 60

1: Using colors and stitches indicated, work A-L (one F and eight G pieces on opposite side of canvas) pieces according to graphs and stitch pattern guides. Using white and Scotch Stitch over three bars (see Stitch Illustration), work M.

2: With matching colors, Overcast unfinished edges of A-G pieces and K pieces as indicated on graph. Using pearl cotton or six strands floss, Backstitch and Straight Stitch, embroider detail as indicated on A, B and I graphs.

3: With beading needle and matching color threads, sew beads and heart buttons to A and I pieces as indicated.

4: Using tan and Herringbone Whipstitch (see Stitch Illustration on page 67), Whipstitch H-K pieces together through all thicknesses according to Box Assembly Diagram. With white, Whipstitch L-N pieces together according to Lid Assembly Diagram.

5: Matching edges, glue O pieces together and to wrong side of A; glue A to box front as shown in

Canister Lid
Stitch Pattern Guide

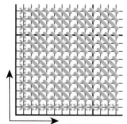

Continue established pattern up and across entire piece.

Canister Front & Bottom
Stitch Pattern Guide

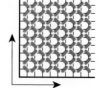

Continue established pattern up and across entire piece.

**K – Canister
Corner Brace**
(cut 4) 8 x 8 holes

Overcast

**A – Canister
Front Facade**
(cut 1)
51 x 59 holes

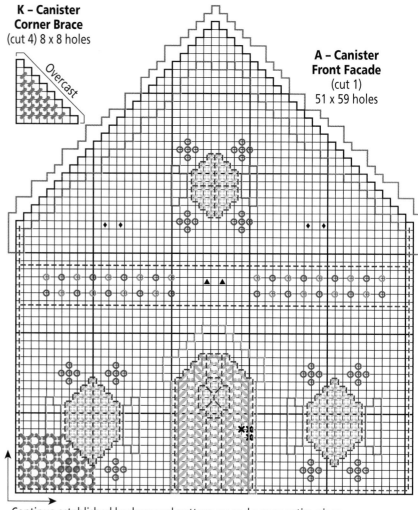

Continue established background pattern up and across entire piece.

**F – Canister
Small Shutter**
(cut 2)
2 x 5 holes

**G – Canister
Large Shutter**
(cut 16)
2 x 7 holes

**D – Canister
Roof Snow**
(cut 1) 31 x 53 holes

E – Canister Chimney Snow
(cut 1) 6 x 11 holes

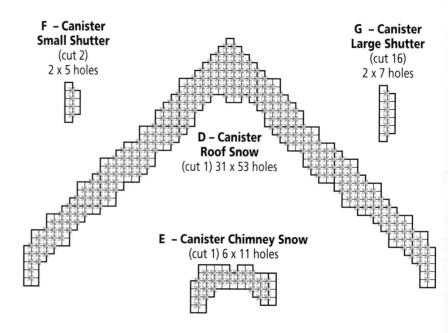

photo. Glue door frame, snow and shutters to Canister as indicated; glue chimney to back of front facade as shown.

DOORSTOP CUTTING INSTRUCTIONS

NOTE: Use 7-count canvas throughout.

A-F: Follow Steps A-F of Canister on page 60.

G: For large shutters, cut four according to Canister G graph.

H: For cover sides, cut two 26 x 55 holes (no graph).

I: For cover ends, cut two 16 x 26 holes (no graph).

J: For cover top and bottom, cut two (one for top and one for bottom) 16 x 55 holes (no graph).

K: For candy canes, cut four 5 x 29 holes.

L: Follow Step O of Canister.

STITCHING INSTRUCTIONS

1: Using colors and stitches indicated, work A-G (one F and two G pieces on opposite side of canvas) pieces according to Cookie Canister A-G graphs; work H-J pieces according to Canister Front & Bottom Stitch Pattern Guide. Using colors indicated and Continental Stitch, work K pieces according to graph.

2: With matching colors, Overcast unfinished edges of A-G pieces. Using pearl cotton or six strands floss,

Backstitch and Straight Stitch, embroider detail as indicated on A and B graphs. With beading needle and matching threads, sew remaining buttons and beads to A as indicated.

Continued on page 70

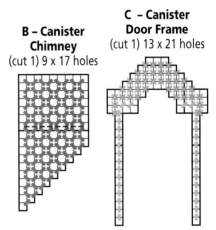

B – Canister Chimney
(cut 1) 9 x 17 holes

C – Canister Door Frame
(cut 1) 13 x 21 holes

Box Assembly Diagram

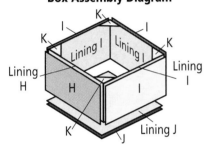

Scotch Stitch Illustration

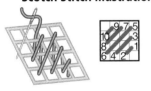

K – Doorstop Candy Cane
(cut 4) 5 x 29 holes

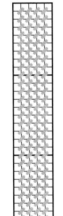

Lid Assembly Diagram
(Pieces are shown in different colors for contrast.)

Step 1:
For handle base, holding unworked N pieces together and to center of lining M, with white, Whipstitch together through all thicknesses.

Step 2:
For handle, holding lining M to wrong side of worked M, Whipstitch together.

Step 4:
Holding lining L to wrong side of worked L, Whipstitch together.

Step 3:
Tack handle base to center right side of worked L.

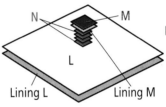

CANISTER & DOORSTOP COLOR KEY:

#3 pearl cotton			Amount
■ Brown			8 yds.

Worsted-weight	Nylon Plus™	Need-loft®	Yarn Amount
■ Camel	#34	#43	3 oz.
□ White	#01	#41	40 yds.
■ Red	#19	#02	15 yds.
□ Yellow	#26	#56	12 yds.
■ Cinnamon	#44	#14	5 yds.
■ Black	#02	#00	1/2 yd.

STITCH KEY:

- — Backstitch/Straight Stitch
- □ Door Frame Placement
- □ Roof Snow Placement
- □ Small Shutter Placement
- □ Large Shutter Placement
- O Bead Attachment
- ▲ Small Button Attachment
- ♦ Large Button Attachment

I – Canister Side (cut 3) 31 x 51 holes

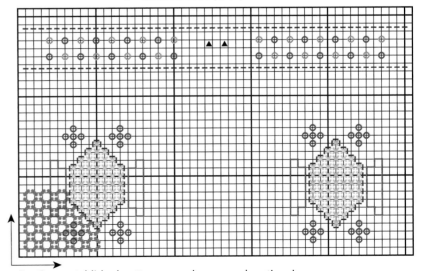

Continue established pattern up and across each entire piece.

Gingerbread Village Continued from page 69

3: Using camel and Herringbone Whipstitch (see Stitch Illustration on page 67), Whipstitch H-J pieces together (insert zip-close bag before closing), forming cover. For each Candy Cane, holding two K pieces wrong sides together, with white, Whipstitch together.

4: Matching edges, glue L pieces together and to wrong side of A; glue A to one side of cover as shown in photo. Glue door frame, snow and shutters to Doorstop as indicated; glue chimney to back of front facade as shown.

COASTERS & HOLDER CUTTING INSTRUCTIONS

NOTES: Use 10-count canvas throughout.

A: For Coasters, cut four according to graph.

B: For Holder front and sides, cut four (two for front and two for sides) according to graph.

C: For Holder back, cut one according to graph.

COASTERS & HOLDER COLOR KEY:

#3 pearl cotton or floss	Amount
☐ Tan	48 yds.
☐ White	43 yds.
■ Red	18 yds.
■ Green	15 yds.
■ Brown	12 yds.
☐ Yellow	10 yds.
■ Blue	6 yds.
■ Gold	6 yds.

#5 pearl cotton or floss	Amount
■ White	7 yds.
☐ Red	5 yds.

STITCH KEY:
— Backstitch/Straight Stitch

D: For Holder bottom, cut one 17 x 46 holes (no graph).

E: For candy canes, cut six according to graph.

F: For Coaster backings, using one A as a pattern, cut four from corkboard ⅛" smaller at all edges.

G: For Holder felt linings, using each B-D piece as a pattern, cut one of each from felt ⅛" smaller at all edges.

H: For Holder cardboard linings, using each B-D piece as a pattern, cut one of each from cardboard ⅛" smaller at all edges.

STITCHING INSTRUCTIONS

NOTES: Use Continental Stitch unless otherwise stated. If using floss, use six strands for embroidery.

1: For Coasters, using #3 pearl cotton or twelve strands floss in col-

E – Candy Cane
(cut 6) 10 x 13 holes

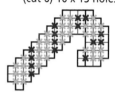

A – Coaster
(cut 4)
46 x 51 holes

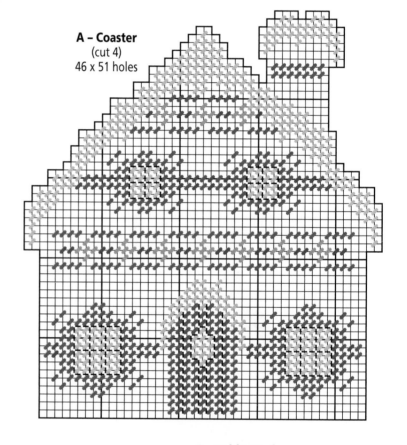

B – Holder Front & Side
(cut 4) 17 x 18 holes

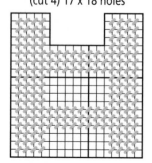

Holder Assembly Diagram

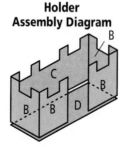

C – Holder Back
(cut 1)
18 x 46 holes

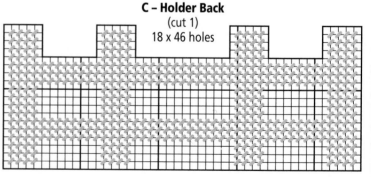

ors indicated, work A pieces according to graph; fill in uncoded areas using tan. With matching colors as shown in photo, Overcast unfinished edges. Using brown and Backstitch, embroider as indicated on graph. Glue one F to back of each A.

2: For Holder, using #3 pearl cotton or twelve strands white floss, work B and C pieces according to graphs; fill in uncoded areas and work D using tan. Using #5 pearl cotton or six strands floss in colors indicated and Cross Stitch, work E pieces according to graph; with white, Overcast unfinished edges.

3: With #3 pearl cotton or twelve strands white floss, Whipstitch B-D pieces together according to Holder Assembly Diagram; Overcast unfinished edges. For linings, glue matching G and H pieces together; glue cardboard side of linings to wrong side of matching B-D pieces (see photo). Glue candy canes to Holder as shown.❈

Ribbon Candy Bow Instructions on page 62

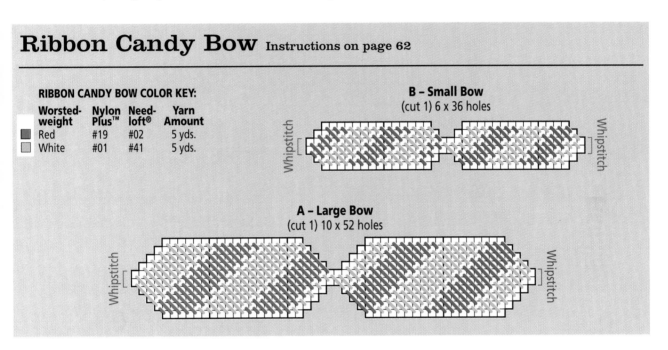

RIBBON CANDY BOW COLOR KEY:

	Worsted-weight	Nylon Plus™	Need-loft®	Yarn Amount
Red		#19	#02	5 yds.
White		#01	#41	5 yds.

B – Small Bow
(cut 1) 6 x 36 holes

Whipstitch   Whipstitch

A – Large Bow
(cut 1) 10 x 52 holes

Whipstitch   Whipstitch

Remembrance Poinsettia Instructions on page 62

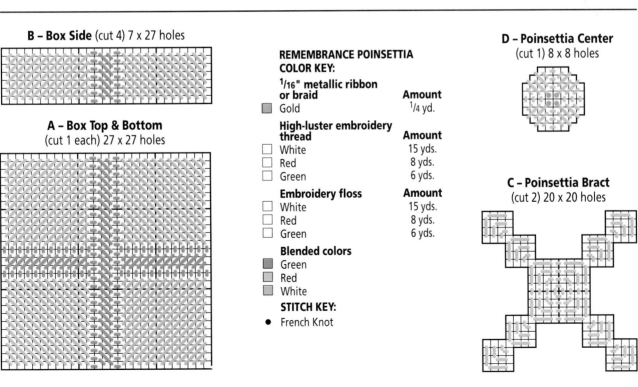

B – Box Side (cut 4) 7 x 27 holes

A – Box Top & Bottom
(cut 1 each) 27 x 27 holes

REMEMBRANCE POINSETTIA COLOR KEY:

	1/16" metallic ribbon or braid	Amount
	Gold	1/4 yd.

	High-luster embroidery thread	Amount
	White	15 yds.
	Red	8 yds.
	Green	6 yds.

	Embroidery floss	Amount
	White	15 yds.
	Red	8 yds.
	Green	6 yds.

Blended colors
Green
Red
White

STITCH KEY:
● French Knot

D – Poinsettia Center
(cut 1) 8 x 8 holes

C – Poinsettia Bract
(cut 2) 20 x 20 holes

Snow is Glistening

Create your own winter wonderland
with projects that will warm your
heart despite the weather. Frosty
and family pose for a cross stitch
sampler while some of their kin
liven a perky blue and white
kitchen set. Using techniques ranging
from thread crochet to shadow
appliqué, you'll quickly pass those
long winter nights stitching
to your heart's content.

Fairyland Forest

Designed by Jo Ann Maxwell

TECHNIQUE:
• Crochet

SIZE:
• Large Tree is 6" tall
• Medium Tree is 5" tall
• Small Tree is 4" tall

MATERIALS:
• Size 10 bedspread cotton — 500 yds. white
• Liquid fabric stiffener
• Drinking straw
• Plastic wrap
• No. 5 steel crochet hook or size needed to obtain gauge

GAUGE:
• 3 dc rows = 1"

LARGE TREE

NOTE: Work in **back lps** unless otherwise stated.

Rnd 1: Ch 4, 20 dc in 4th ch from hook, join with sl st in top of ch-3 (21 dc).

Rnd 2: Ch 3, dc in each st around, join.

Rnd 3: Ch 3, dc in each of next 2 sts, (2 dc in next st, dc in next st) around, join (30).

Rnd 4: Ch 3, dc in each st around, join.

Rnd 5: Ch 3, dc in each of next 2 sts, 2 dc in next st, (dc in next st, 2 dc in next st) around, join (44).

Rnds 6-9: Ch 3, dc in each st around, join.

Rnd 10: Ch 3, dc in same st, 2 dc in next st, (dc in each of next 2 sts, 2 dc in next st) around, join (60).

Rnd 11: Ch 3, dc in each st around, join.

Rnd 12: Ch 3, dc in each of next 3 sts, (2 dc in next st, dc in next 6 sts) around, join (68).

Rnd 13: Ch 3, dc in each st around, join.

Rnd 14: Ch 3, 2 dc in next st, (dc in next 5 sts, 2 dc in next st) around, join (80).

Rnds 15-18: Ch 3, dc in each st around, join. At end of last rnd, fasten off.

BRANCHES

NOTE: For **shell,** (2 dc, ch 2, 2 dc) in next st or ch sp.

Rnd 1: Working in **front lps** of rnd 1, with top of Tree facing you, join with sl st in any st, (ch 3, dc, ch 2, 2 dc) in same st, ch 1, skip next 2 sts, (shell in next st, ch 1, skip next 2 sts) around, join with sl st in top of ch-3.

NOTE: For **triple picot (tr-picot),** (ch 5, sl st, ch 7, sl st, ch 5, sl st) in top of last st made.

Rnd 2: Sl st in next st, (sl st, ch 3, 2 dc, tr-picot, 2 dc) in next ch sp, ch 1, sc in next ch-1 sp, ch 1, *(3 dc, tr-picot, 2 dc) in ch sp of next shell, ch 1, sc in next ch-1 sp, ch 1; repeat from * around, join, fasten off.

Repeat Branches in **front lps** of rnd 4. Skipping 3 sts instead of 2 in rnd 1, repeat Branches in **front lps** of rnds 7, 10, 13 and 16.

MEDIUM TREE

Rnds 1-15: Repeat same rnds of Large Tree. At end of last rnd, fasten off.

BRANCHES

Work same as Large Tree's Branches.

Repeat Branches in **front lps** of rnd 4. Skipping 3 sts instead of 2 in rnd 1, repeat Branches in **front lps** of rnds 7, 10 and 13.

SMALL TREE

Rnds 1-12: Repeat same rnds of Large Tree. At end of last rnd, fasten off.

BRANCHES

Work same as Large Tree's Branches.

Repeat Branches in **front lps** of rnd 4. Skipping 3 sts instead of 2 in rnd 1, repeat Branches in **front lps** of rnds 7 and 10.

FINISHING

1: For form, scrunch up layers of plastic wrap and shape around straw to form a cone. Cover entire cone with another layer of wrap.

2: For each Tree, apply fabric stiffener according to manufacturer's instructions. Place over form. Shape Branches as piece dries.❈

Frosty & Family

Designed by Nancy Marshall

STITCHING INSTRUCTIONS

1: Center and stitch design, using two strands floss or two strands floss held together with one strand blending filament for Cross Stitch. Use one strand floss for Backstitch of snowcaps on letters and snow fall on small trees. Use two strands floss for remaining Backstitch.❄

Graph continued on page 84

TECHNIQUE:
• Cross Stitch

MATERIALS:
• 14" x 16" piece of white 14-count Aida

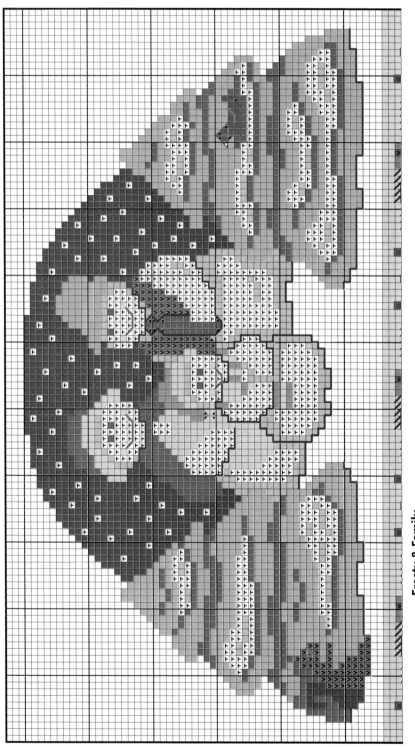

Frosty & Family

X	B'st	¹/₄x	³/₄x	DMC	ANCHOR	J.&P. COATS	COLORS	KREINIK(BF)
				#310	#403	#8403	Black	
				#317	#400	#8512	Darkest Silver	
				#318	#399	#8511	Silver Med.	
				#318	#399	#8511	Silver Med. held together with	#032 Pearl
				#321	#9046	#3500	Cherry Red	
				#434	#310	#5000	Darkest Toast	
				#436	#1045	#5943	Toast	
				#741	#304	#2314	Tangerine Dk.	
				#743	#302	#2294	Tangerine Lt.	
				#797	#132	#7143	Deep Blueberry	
				#801	#359	#5472	Coffee Brown Dk.	
				#813	#161	#7161	Sky Blue Med.	
				#909	#923	#6228	Green Dk.	
				#912	#209	#6266	Seafoam Green Dk.	
				#3326	#36	#3126	Rose Pink	
				White	#2	#1001	White	
				White	#2	#1001	White held together with	#032 Pearl

Ice Medallions

Designed by Roberta A. Maier

TECHNIQUE:
• Crochet

SIZE:
• Each Medallion is 2" across
• Pot Holder is 7½" across

MATERIALS:
• Size 10 bedspread cotton — 70 yds. white
• Cotton worsted-weight yarn — 50 yds. red and 5 yds. white
• Tapestry needle
• No. 8 steel and G crochet hooks or sizes needed to obtain gauges

GAUGES:
• No. 8 steel hook, rnd 1 of Medallion = ¾" across
• G hook, 4 sc = 1"; 4 sc rnds = 1"

MEDALLION (make 7)

Rnd 1: With No. 8 hook and bedspread cotton, ch 10, sl st in first ch to form ring, ch 3, 17 dc in ring, join with sl st in top of ch-3 (18 dc).

Rnd 2: Ch 1, sc in first st, (*ch 4, tr next 2 sts tog, ch 4*, sc in next st) 5 times; repeat between **, join with sl st in first sc.

Rnd 3: Sl st in first ch-4 sp, ch 1, 5 sc in same sp, *(sc, ch 5, sc) in next st, 5 sc in each of next 2 ch-4 sps; repeat from * 4 more times, (sc, ch 3, sc) in next st, 5 sc in last ch-4 sp, join, fasten off.

POT HOLDER
FRONT

NOTE: Do not join rnds unless otherwise stated. Mark first st of each rnd.

Rnd 1: With G hook and red, ch 4, sl st in first ch to form ring, ch 1, 8 sc in ring (8 sc).

Rnd 2: 2 sc in each st around (16).

Rnd 3: (Sc in next st, 2 sc in next st) around (24).

Rnd 4: Holding wrong side of one Medallion to right side of Front, working through both thicknesses, sc in one ch-5 sp on Medallion and next st on rnd 3 at same time, sc in each of next 3 sts, (sc in next ch-5 sp on Medallion and next st on rnd 3, sc in each of next 3 sts) around.

Rnds 5-6: Repeat rnd 3 (36, 54).

Rnds 7-8: Sc in each st around.

Rnd 9: (Sc in each of next 2 sts, 2 sc in next st) around (72).

Rnds 10-11: Sc in each st around.

Rnd 12: Holding wrong side of one Medallion to right side of Front, working through both thicknesses, sc in one ch-5 sp on Medallion and next st on rnd 11, (sc in each of next 3 sts, sc in next ch-5 on same Medallion and next st on rnd 11, sc in next 7 sts, (sc in one ch-5 sp on next Medallion and next st on rnd 11, sc in each of next 3 sts, sc in next ch-5 sp on same Medallion and next st on rnd 11, sc in next 7 sts) around.

Rnd 13: Repeat rnd 9, join with sl st in first sc, fasten off (96).

Tack unworked ch-5 sps on each Medallion to Pot Holder Front.

Continued on page 85

Frosted Crystal Pillow

Designed by Charlyne Stewart

INSTRUCTIONS

NOTE: From pindot fabric, cut one 15½" square for front shadow square, one 17" square, two 2" x 15½" strips and two 2" x 17" strips. From sheer fabric, cut one 15½" square. From fleece, cut one 14" square. From tissue paper, cut one same as fleece. From cardboard, cut one same as fleece and one 7" square.

1: For snowflake, trace Snowflake pattern on page 85 onto 7" square piece of cardboard; cut out. Fold tissue paper into eight equal sections (see Folding Diagram on page 85.) Trace cardboard pattern onto tissue paper according to Step 4 of Folding Diagram; cut out and unfold. Trace tissue paper pattern onto fleece; cut out.

2: With right side of 15½" square fabric piece and wrong side of sheer 15½" square fabric together and with fleece snowflake centered between, pin together. Working through all layers and using small Running Stitches (see illustration on page 85), quilt around outside and cutout edges of snowflake, forming shadow square. Sew one each 2" x 15½" fabric strips to top and bottom and one each 2" x 17" fabric strip to each side of shadow square, forming pillow front. With right sides of front and back together, sew together, leaving one side open; turn right sides out. Insert pillow form; slip stitch opening closed.

3: For tassel (make four), cut 3½" x 5" piece of cardboard. Holding 6" length of yarn along top of cardboard, wind yarn around short width of cardboard twenty-eight times. Tie short length of yarn around

Continued on page 85

TECHNIQUE:
• Sewing/Shadow Appliqué

SIZE:
• 16" square

MATERIALS:
• 16" square pillow form
• ½ yd. red pindot cotton fabric
• ½ yd. sheer fabric
• ½ yd. white fleece
• One skein red 4-ply yarn
• Red quilting and sewing thread
• 14" square piece of thin tissue paper
• Cardboard
• Tracing paper

TECHNIQUE:
- Crochet

SIZE:
- 4" Sole

MATERIALS:
- Pompadour baby yarn — 1 oz. white
- Sport yarn — small amount each black and red
- Small amount orange size 10 bedspread cotton
- Tapestry needle
- No. 5 steel crochet hook or size needed to obtain gauge

GAUGE:
- 7 dc sts = 1"
- 3 dc rows = 1"

Jollytime Booties

Designed by Kathleen Stuart

BOOTIE (make 2)
SOLE & SIDES

Rnd 1: Starting at **heel,** with white, ch 18, 3 dc in 4th ch from hook, dc in next 13 chs, 8 dc in last ch; working on opposite side of ch, dc in next 13 chs, 4 dc in last ch, join with sl st in top of ch-3 (42 dc).

Rnd 2: Ch 1, 2 sc in each of first 3 sts, sc in next 5 sts, hdc in next st, dc in next 9 sts, 2 dc in each of next 6 sts, dc in next 9 sts, hdc in next st, sc in next 5 sts, 2 sc in each of last 3 sts, join with sl st in first sc (54 sts).

Rnd 3: Ch 3, dc in same st, 2 dc in each of next 3 sts, dc in next 19 sts, 2 dc in each of next 8 sts, dc in next 19 sts, 2 dc in each of last 4 sts, join with sl st in top of ch-3 (70 dc).

Rnd 4: Working this rnd in **back lps** only, ch 3, dc in each st around, join.

Rnd 5: Ch 3, dc in each st around, join.

Rnd 6: Ch 3, dc in next 28 sts, (dc next 2 sts tog) 6 times, dc in each st around, join, fasten off (64).

INSTEP

Row 1: Working in 7 center sts on toe, join white with sc in first st, sc in next 6 sts, turn (7 sc).

Rows 2-15: Ch 1, sc in first 7 sc, skip next st on Side, sl st in next st, turn. (Sl st is not used or counted as a st). At end of last row, fasten off.

TOP HAT

Rnd 1: Working around top opening in **back lps** only, join black with sl st in center back st, ch 3, dc in each st around, join with sl st in top of ch-3 (36 dc).

Rnds 2-3: Ch 3, dc in each st around, join. At end of last rnd, fasten off.

Rnd 4: For **brim,** working in **front lps** around top opening with opening toward you, join black with sl st in center back st, ch 3, 2 dc in next st, (dc in next st, 2 dc in next st) around, join, fasten off.

HATBAND

With red, leaving 6" end, ch 40, fasten off leaving 6" end. Place around rnd 1 of Hat; tie 6" ends in bow at front. Tack in place.

NOSE

Rnd 1: With orange, ch 2, 6 sc in 2nd ch from hook, **do not** join (6 sc).

Rnds 2-5: Sc in each st around, **do not** join. At end of last rnd, join with sl st in first sc, fasten off.

Sew Nose to center of Instep. With black, using French Knot, embroider eyes above Nose and mouth below Nose as shown in photo.❄

Snowflake Topper

Designed by Jo Ann Maxwell

LARGE SNOWFLAKE

Rnd 1: Ch 4, sl st in first ch to form ring, ch 3, 23 dc in ring, join with sl st in top of ch-3 (24 dc).

Rnd 2: (Ch 25, sl st, ch 30, sl st, ch 25, sl st) in first st, *sl st in next 4 sts, (ch 25, sl st, ch 30, sl st, ch 25, sl st) in same st as last sl st; repeat from * 4 more times, sl st in each of last 3 sts, join with sl st in joining sl st of last rnd, fasten off.

MEDIUM SNOWFLAKE

Rnd 1: Repeat same rnd of Large Snowflake.

Rnd 2: (Ch 20, sl st, ch 25, sl st, ch 20, sl st) in first st, *sl st in next 4 sts, (ch 20, sl st, ch 25, sl st, ch 20, sl st) in same st as last sl st; repeat from * 4 more times, sl st in each of last 3 sts, join with sl st in joining sl st of last rnd, fasten off.

SMALL SNOWFLAKE

Ch 4, sl st in first ch to form ring, (ch 15, sl st in ring, ch 20, sl st in ring, ch 15, sl st in ring) 6 times, fasten off.

FINISHING

1: Apply fabric stiffener to Snowflakes according to manufacturer's instructions. Pin flat on foam or cutting board. Let dry.

2: Glue Medium Snowflake to center of Large Snowflake. Glue Small Snowflake to center of Medium Snowflake. Glue stone to center of Small Snowflake.

3: Glue assembled Snowflakes to one side of headband.❄

TECHNIQUE:
• Crochet

SIZE:
• Snowflake is 5" across

MATERIALS:
• Size 10 bedspread cotton — 50 yds. white
• 10-mm x 15-mm oval acrylic stone
• White plastic head-band
• Liquid fabric stiffener
• Rust-free pins
• Styrofoam® or cutting board
• Craft glue or hot glue gun
• No. 7 steel crochet hook or size needed to obtain gauge

GAUGE:
• 4 chs = ½"

Snowman Kitchen

Designed by Angela J. Tate

SNOWMAN (make 6)

Rnd 1: With white, ch 4, sl st in first ch to form ring, ch 3, 14 dc in ring, join with sl st in top of ch-3 (15 dc).

Rnd 2: Ch 3, dc in same st, 2 dc in each st around, join (30).

Row 3: For **Head,** working in rows, ch 3, dc in same st, dc in each of next 2 sts, 2 dc in next st leaving remaining sts unworked, turn (6 dc).

Row 4: Ch 3, dc in each st across, fasten off.

Cut 8" strand of red, tie into a bow around two center sts of rnd 2 at neck.

From felt, cut nose and circles according to pattern pieces. Glue to Snowman as shown in photo.

HAT (make 6)

Row 1: With green, ch 11, sc in 2nd ch from hook, sc in each ch across, turn (10 sc).

Row 2: Sl st in first 4 sts, ch 3, dc in each of next 3 sts leaving remaining sts unworked, turn (4).

Row 3: Ch 3, dc in each st across, fasten off.

With red, using Chain Stitch (see Stitch Guide), embroider hatband across row 2 of Hat.

PLACE MAT (make 4)

Row 1: With blue, ch 55, dc in 4th ch from hook, dc in each ch across, turn (53 dc).

Rows 2-19: Ch 3, dc in each st across, turn. At end of last row, **do not** turn, fasten off.

Rnd 20: Working around outer edge in ends of rows and in sts, join white with sl st in any st, ch 3, dc in each st and 2 dc in each row around with 5 dc in each corner, join with sl st in top of ch-3, fasten off.

Sew or glue one Snowman and Hat to bottom right-hand corner.

POT HOLDER SIDE (make 2)

Row 1: With blue, ch 23, dc in 4th ch from hook, dc in each ch across, turn (21 dc).

Rows 2-12: Ch 3, dc in each st across, turn. At end of last row, **do not** turn, fasten off.

Rnd 20: Hold Sides together, matching sts; working through both thicknesses in ends of rows and in sts around outer edge, join white with sl st in upper left-hand corner, (ch 3, dc) in same corner; for **hanging loop,** ch 10, sl st in first ch to form ring, ch 1, sc in each ch of hanging lp, sl st in last dc made, 2 dc in same corner, sc in each st and 2 dc in each row around with 5 dc in each corner, join with sl st in top of ch-3, fasten off.

Sew or glue one Snowman and Hat to center of Pot Holder.

TOWEL HOLDER

Row 1: With blue, ch 50, sl st in first ch to form ring, ch 3, dc in first 20 chs leaving remaining chs unworked, turn (21 dc).

Rows 2-12: Ch 3, dc in each st across, turn.

Row 13: Sl st in first 8 sts, ch 3, dc in next 6 sts leaving remaining sts unworked, turn (7 dc).

Rows 14-20: Ch 3, dc in each st across, turn. At end of last row, **do not** turn, fasten off.

Rnd 21: Working in starting ch around bottom opening, join blue with sc in any ch, sc in each ch around, join with sl st in first sc, fasten off.

Rnd 22: Working around outer edge in ends of rows and in sts, join white with sl st in any st, ch 3, dc in each st, in each ch and 2 dc in each row around with 5 dc in each end of rows 12 and 20, join with sl st in top of ch-3, fasten off.

Sew or glue one Snowman and Hat to front. Sew button centered to row 20 on back side, using sps between sts on row 14 for buttonhole.

Press each long edge of fabric under ⅛", sew long edges and one short end to Holder centered below bottom opening on wrong side. Holding craft sticks together as one, slide inside.✿

NOSE PATTERN PIECE
Cut 1 from orange felt
(actual size)

CIRCLE PATTERN PIECE
Cut 5 from black felt
(actual size)

TECHNIQUE:
• Crochet

SIZE:
• Place Mat is 11½" x 17½"
• Pot Holder is 7½" x 8¼"
• Towel Holder is 7½" x 11¼"

MATERIALS FOR ENTIRE SET:
• Worsted-weight yarn— 14 oz. blue, 4 oz. fuzzy white, small amount each green and red
• Scraps of black and orange felt
• 1" x 5" scrap white fabric
• ¾" white button
• Two ⅜" x 4½" craft sticks
• White sewing thread
• Craft glue or hot glue gun
• Sewing and tapestry needles
• I crochet hook or size needed to obtain gauge

GAUGE:
• 3 dc sts = 1"
• 5 dc rows = 3"

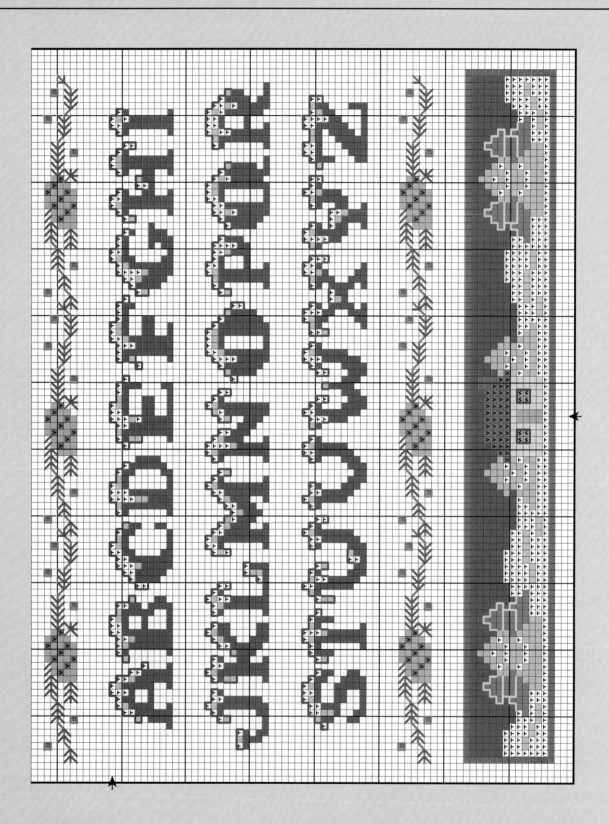

Frosty & Family

X	B'st	1/4x	3/4x	DMC	ANCHOR	J&P COATS	COLORS	KREINIK(BF)
				#310	#403	#8403	Black	
				#317	#400	#8512	Darkest Silver	
				#318	#399	#8511	Silver Med.	
				#318	#399	#8511	Silver Med. held together with	#032 Pearl
				#321	#9046	#3500	Cherry Red	
				#434	#310	#5000	Darkest Toast	
				#436	#1045	#5943	Toast	
				#741	#304	#2314	Tangerine Dk.	
				#743	#302	#2294	Tangerine Lt.	
				#797	#132	#7143	Deep Blueberry	
				#801	#359	#5472	Coffee Brown Dk.	
				#813	#161	#7161	Sky Blue Med.	
				#909	#923	#6228	Green Dk.	
				#912	#209	#6266	Seafoam Green Dk.	
				#3326	#36	#3126	Rose Pink	
				White	#2	#1001	White	
				White	#2	#1001	White held together with	#032 Pearl

Ice Medallions

Continued from page 78

BACK

Rnds 1-3: Repeat same rnds of Front.
Rnd 4: Sc in each st around.
Rnds 5-11: Repeat same rnds of Front.
Rnd 12: Sc in each st around.
Rnd 13: Repeat rnd 9 of Front, join with sl st in first sc, fasten off (96).

BORDER

Hold Front and Back wrong sides together with front facing you, matching sts; working through both thicknesses, with G hook and white worsted-weight, join with sc in any st, sc in each st around, join with sl st in first sc; for **hanging loop**, ch 15, sl st in same st, **turn,** sl st in each ch of ch-15, fasten off.❄

Frosted Crystal Pillow

Continued from page 79

tassel ¾" from tied end. Trim ends of tassel; tack one tassel to each corner of pillow.❄

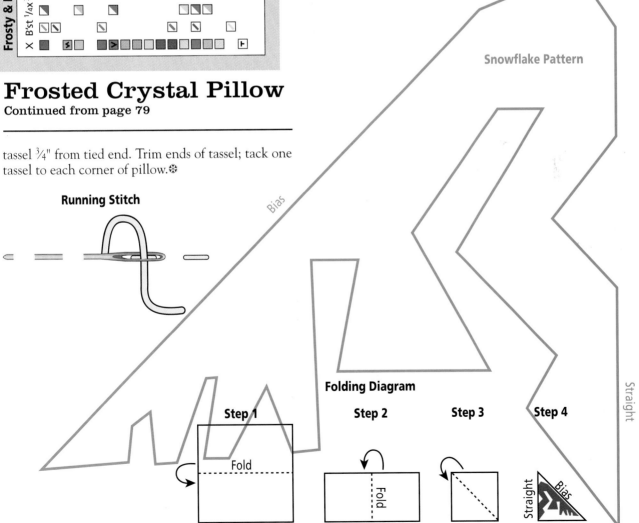

Running Stitch

Snowflake Pattern

Bias

Straight

Folding Diagram

Step 1 — Fold

Step 2 — Fold

Step 3

Step 4 — Straight / Bias

Dreaming by the Fire

Deck the halls and stoke the fire,
then sit back and relax in a toasty,
holiday atmosphere glowing with
cheerful handcrafted goodies.
Even old Saint Nick himself couldn't
have come up with a better
assortment of gift and home decor
ideas. Rich with the traditional
motifs of poinsettias and holly, these
distinctive, yet touchable projects
will easily be tops on your list.

Gilded Poinsettias

Designed by Teresa S. Hannaway

CUTTING INSTRUCTIONS

1: From fabric No. 1, cut sixteen pieces using pattern A and one 31½" x 31½" piece for back.

2: From fabric No. 2, cut thirty-six pieces using pattern A and four 3¼" x 31½" strips for outer border.

3: From fabric No. 3, cut twenty pieces using pattern A.

4: From fabric No. 4, cut twenty pieces using pattern B and four 1¼" x 31½" strips for inner border.

5: From fabric No. 5, cut twenty pieces using pattern B.

6: From fabrics No. 6 and No. 7, cut sixteen pieces each using pattern B.

7: From fusible fleece, cut one 31" x 31" piece.

PIECING INSTRUCTIONS

NOTE: All seams are ¼" unless otherwise noted.

1: For piecing, with right sides together and following color numbers, sew A pattern pieces into strips according to Piecing Diagram on page 98; press seams. With right sides together, sew long edges of strips together, forming front piece.

2: Apply pattern B fabric pieces, using fusible webbing (see Poinsettia Assembly Diagram on page 98) according to Front Assembly Diagram on page 98 and following manufacturer's instructions. Apply fusible fleece to wrong side of front piece following manufacturer's instructions.

3: Carefully apply glitter paint to edges of pattern B fabric pieces. Allow to dry. Sew six red beads to center of each brown poinsettia and six gold beads to center of each red poinsettia as shown in photo.

4: With right sides together, sew one long edge of each inner border strip to one long edge of each outer border strip. With right sides together, sew one inner border to each edge of front piece ending ¼" from each corner. Miter corners according to Mitering Illustration on page 98.

5: With right sides together, sew front and back together leaving an opening. Turn right sides out; slip stitch opening closed.✤

TECHNIQUE:
• Sewing

SIZE:
• 29" square

MATERIALS:
• 1¼ yds. med. green fabric (No. 1)
• ¾ yd. poinsettia floral fabric (No. 2)
• ⅓ yd. dk. green fabric (No. 3)
• ⅓ yd. dk. red fabric (No. 4)
• ¼ yd. med. red fabric (No. 5)
• ¼ yd. med. brown fabric (No. 6)
• ¼ yd. lt. brown fabric (No. 7)
• Fusible fleece
• Fusible webbing
• 30 gold 6-mm faceted beads
• 24 red 6-mm faceted beads
• Gold glitter fabric paint

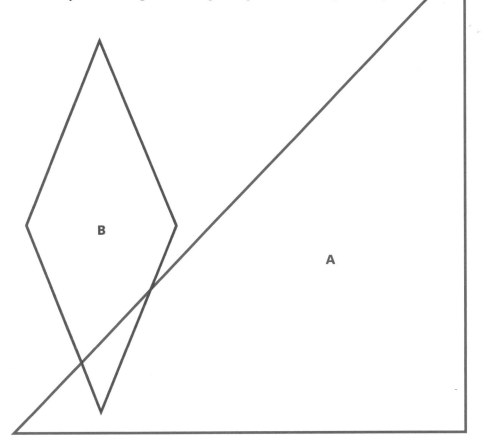

Christmas Coveralls

Designed by Rosanne Kropp

TECHNIQUE:
• Crochet

SIZE:
• Instructions given fit infant's 6 mos.
• Changes for child's sizes 1 and 2 are in [ ]

MATERIALS:
• Sport yarn — 8 [8, 10] oz. green, 3 oz. each white and red
• 10 [12, 13] red ½" buttons
• Red sewing thread
• Sewing and tapestry needles
• E and F crochet hooks or sizes needed to obtain gauges

GAUGES:
• E hook, 5 sc = 1"; 4 back lp sc rows = 1"
• F hook, 4 hdc sts = 1"; 3 hdc rows = 1"

FIRST LEG

Row 1: Starting at cuff, with E hook and green, ch 7, sc in 2nd ch from hook, sc in each ch across, turn (6 sc).

Rows 2-25 [2-27, 2-29]: Working these rows in **back lps,** ch 1, sc in each st across, turn. At end of last row, **do not** turn.

Row 26 [28, 30]: Working in ends of rows, with F hook, ch 1, 2 hdc in first row, (hdc in next row, 2 hdc in next row) across, turn (38 hdc) [41 hdc, 44 hdc].

NOTE: Ch-1 is not used or counted as a stitch.

Rows 27-37 [29-43, 31-48]: Ch 1, hdc in each st across, turn.

Rows 38-41 [44-48, 49-54]: Ch 1, 2 hdc in first st, hdc in each st across, turn, ending with (42) [46, 50] sts in last row.

Rows 42-43 [49-50, 55-60]: Ch 1, 2 hdc in first st, hdc in each st across with 2 hdc in last st, turn, ending with (46) [50, 54] sts in last row. At end of last row, fasten off.

SECOND LEG

Work same as First Leg.

BACK

Row 1: With wrong side of last row on one Leg facing you, join green with sl st in 24th [26th, 28th] st, ch 1, hdc in same st, hdc in next 22 [24, 26] sts; working across other Leg, hdc in next 24 [25, 27] sts leaving remaining sts unworked, turn (46 hdc) [50 hdc, 54 hdc].

Rows 2-11 [2-13, 2-15]: Ch 1, hdc in each st across, turn.

Row 12 [14, 16]: Ch 1, hdc first 2 sts tog, hdc in each st across to last 2 sts, hdc last 2 sts tog, turn (44) [48, 52].

Rows 13-15 [15-17, 17-19]: Ch 1, hdc in each st across, turn.

Rows 16-19 [18-25, 20-27]: Repeat rows 12-15 [14-17, 16-19] consecutively, ending with (42) [44, 48] hdc in last row.

Row 20 [26, 28]: Repeat row 12 [14, 16], ending with (40) [42, 46] sts.

Row 21 [27, 29]: For **underarm,** sl st in each of first 2 [2, 3] sts, ch 1, hdc last worked st and next st tog, hdc in each st across to last 3 [3, 4] sts, hdc next 2 sts tog leaving last 1 [1, 2] sts unworked, turn (36 hdc) [38 hdc, 40 hdc].

Row 22 [28, 30]: Ch 1, hdc first 2 sts tog, hdc in each st across to last 2 sts, hdc last 2 sts tog, turn (34) [36, 38].

Rows 23-33 [29-41, 31-45]: Ch 1, hdc in each st across, turn.

Row 34 [42, 46]: For **first shoulder,** sl st in each of first 2 [2, 3] sts, sc in each of next 3 sts, hdc in each of next 3 sts, dc in each of next 2 sts, dc next 2 sts tog leaving remaining sts unworked, fasten off (11 sts) [11sts, 12 sts].

Row 34 [42, 46]: For **second shoulder,** skip next 10 [12, 12] unworked sts on row 33 [40, 45], join green with sl st in next st, ch 1, dc same st and next st tog, dc in each of next 2 sts, hdc in each of next 3 sts, sc in each of next 3 sts, sl st in each of last 2 [2, 3] sts, fasten off.

FRONT

Row 1: Join green with sl st in first unworked st on Leg, ch 1, hdc in same st, hdc in each unworked st across both Legs, turn (46 hdc) [50 hdc, 54 hdc].

Rows 2-20 [2-26, 2-28]: Repeat same rows of Back.

Row 21 [27, 29]: For **first side,** sl st in each of first 2 [2, 3] sts, ch 1, hdc last worked st and next st tog, hdc in next 15 [16, 17] sts leaving remaining sts unworked, turn (16 hdc) [17 hdc, 18 hdc].

Row 22 [28, 30]: Ch 1, hdc in each st across to last 2 hdc, hdc last 2 hdc tog, turn (15) [16, 17].

Rows 23-29 [29-37, 31-41]: Ch 1, hdc in each st across, turn.

Row 30 [38, 42]: For **neck,** sl st in each of first 2 [3, 3] sts, ch 1, hdc next 2 sts tog, hdc in last 11 [11 12] sts, turn (12) [12, 13].

Row 31 [39, 43]: Ch 1, hdc in each st across to last 2 sts, hdc last 2 sts tog, turn (11) [11, 12].

Rows 32-33 [40-41, 44-45]: Ch 1, hdc in each st across, turn.

Row 34 [42, 46]: Ch 1, dc in each of first 3 sts, hdc in each of next 3 sts, sc in each of next 3 sts, sl st in each of last 2 [2, 3] sts, fasten off.

Row 21 [27, 29]: For **second side,** skip next 4 unworked sts on row 20 [26, 28], join green with sl st in next st, ch 1, hdc in same st, hdc in next 14 [15, 16] sts, hdc next 2 sts tog leaving last 1 [1, 2] st unworked, turn (16 hdc) [17 hdc, 18 hdc].

Row 22 [28, 30]: Ch 1, hdc first 2 sts tog, hdc in each st across, turn (15) [16, 17].

Rows 23-29 [29-37, 31-41]: Ch 1, hdc in each st across, turn.

Row 30 [38, 42]: Ch 1, hdc in first 11 [11, 12] sts, hdc next 2 sts tog leaving remaining sts unworked, turn (12) [12, 13].

Row 31 [39, 43]: Ch 1, hdc first 2 sts tog, hdc in each st across, turn (11) [11, 12].

Rows 32-33 [40-41, 44-45]: Ch 1, hdc in each st across, turn.

Row 34 [42, 46]: Sl st in each of first 2 [2, 3] sts, ch 1, sc in each of next 3 sts, hdc in each of next 3 sts, dc in each of last 3 sts, fasten off.

Sew shoulder seams.

LEFT NECK PLACKET
Row 1: With F hook and white, join with sc in end of last row on left front, evenly space 10 [11, 14] more sc down rows, turn (11 sc) [12 sc, 15 sc].

Rows 2-3: Ch 1, sc in each st across, turn. At end of last row, fasten off.

RIGHT NECK PLACKET
Rows 1-2: Working on right front, repeat same rows of Left Placket.

Row 3: Ch 1, sc in first st; for buttonhole, ch 1, skip next st; (sc in next 5 sts; for buttonhole, ch 1, skip next st) 1 [1, 2] times, sc in each of last 3 [4, 1] sts, fasten off.

Lapping Right Placket over Left Placket, sew bottom edges of Plackets to bottom of Front opening.

Sew buttons to Left Placket opposite buttonholes.

FRONT LEG PLACKET
Row 1: With F hook and green and wrong side facing you, join with sc on bottom corner st on left Leg, evenly space 59 [72, 83] more sc across to corner st on right Leg, turn (60 sc) [73 sc, 84 sc].

Row 2: Ch 1, sc in each st across, turn.

NOTE: Ch-1 sps on next row are used as buttonholes.

Row 3: Ch 1, sc in each of first 3 sts, ch 1, skip next st, sc in next 4 sts, ch 1, skip next st, (sc in next 8 [7, 8] sts, ch 1, skip next st) 2 [3, 3] times, sc in next 6 [7, 12] sts, (ch 1, skip next st, sc in next 8 [7, 8] sts) 2 [3, 3] times, ch 1, skip next st, sc in next 4 sts, ch 1, skip next st, sc in each of last 3 sts, turn.

Row 4: Ch 1, sc in each st and in each ch sp across, fasten off.

BACK LEG PLACKET
Row 1: With F hook and green and wrong side facing you, join with sc on bottom corner st on right Leg, evenly space 59 [72, 83] more sc around to corner st on left Leg, turn (60 sc) [73 sc, 84 sc].

Rows 2-4: Ch 1, sc in each st across, turn. At end of last row, fasten off.

Sew buttons on Back Leg Placket opposite buttonholes on Front Leg Placket.

SLEEVE (make 2)
Row 1: Starting at cuff, with E hook and red, ch 7, sc in 2nd ch from hook, sc in each ch across, turn (6 sc).

Rows 2-24 [2-26, 2-28]: Working these rows in back lps only, ch 1, sc in each st across, turn. At end of last row, do not turn.

Row 25 [27, 29]: Working in ends of rows, with F hook, ch 1, hdc in first 4 rows, 2 hdc in next row, (hdc in next 4 rows, 2 hdc in next row) 3 [2, 4] times, hdc in each row across, turn, fasten off (28 hdc) [29 hdc, 33 hdc].

Row 26 [28, 30]: Join white with sl st in first st, ch 1, hdc in same st, hdc in each st across, turn.

Continued on page 98

Santa Slippers

Designed by Shep Shepherd

TECHNIQUE:
• Crochet

SIZE:
• Instructions given fit 9" sole
• Changes for 10" sole and 11" sole are in [ ]

MATERIALS:
• Fuzzy worsted-weight yarn — 2 [2½, 3] oz. each red and white
• Tapestry needle
• H crochet hook or size needed to obtain gauge

GAUGE:
• 7 hdc sts = 2"
• 4 hdc rows = 2"

SLIPPER (make 2)

Row 1: With red, ch 33 [37, 41], hdc in 3rd ch from hook, hdc in each ch across, turn (32 hdc) [36 hdc, 40 hdc].

Rows 2-13 [2-14, 2-15]: Ch 2, hdc in each st across, turn. At end of last row, fasten off.

Fold in half lengthwise. Sew ends of rows on one end together for heel. Weave seperate 8" strand of red through ends of rows on opposite end for toe, pull to gather, secure end. Sew 16 [20, 24] sts at toe end together to form instep.

CUFF

Rnd 1: Join white with sl st in center back seam, ch 2, hdc in each st around, join with sl st in top of ch-2.

Rnds 2-3: Ch 2, hdc in each st around, join. At end of last rnd, fasten off.

Rnd 4: Working around post of sts on rnd 1, join with sl st around post of first st, ch 2, 2 hdc around same st, 3 hdc around post of each st around, join, fasten off.

Rnds 5-6: Repeat rnd 4 on rnds 2 and 3.❄

Candy Bucket

Designed by Virginia Hockenbury

TECHNIQUE:
• Plastic Canvas

SIZE:
• 4¼" across x 4¼" tall, not including handle

MATERIALS:
• One sheet of 7-count plastic canvas
• One 18" length of 16-gauge floral wire
• 1 yd. red ¼" satin ribbon
• Worsted-weight or plastic canvas yarn (for amounts see Color Key on page 99)

CUTTING INSTRUCTIONS

NOTE: Graphs on page 99.

A: For side, cut one 27 x 90 holes.

B: For bottom, cut one according to graph.

C: For handle, cut one 13 x 17 holes.

D: For handle ends, cut two according to graph.

STITCHING INSTRUCTIONS

1: Overlapping holes at ends of side and handle as indicated on graphs and working through both thicknesses at overlap areas to join, using colors and stitches indicated, work A-D pieces according to graphs.

2: With red, Whipstitch A and B together; Overcast unfinished edges of side. With green, Whipstitch C and D pieces together, forming handle.

NOTE: Cut ribbon into four 9" lengths.

3: Tie ribbons into bows; trim ends. Glue

Continued on page 99

Pretty Presentation

Designed by Denise Cheek

COVER

Rnd 1: Starting at top, with green, ch 24, sl st in first ch to form ring, ch 3, 2 dc in same ch, dc in next 5 chs, (3 dc in next ch, dc in next 5 chs) around, join with sl st in top of ch-3 (32 dc).

Rnds 2-3: Ch 3, dc in each st around with 3 dc in center st of each 3-dc corner group, join (40, 48).

Rnd 4: Ch 1, (sc in each st across to next 3-dc group, hdc in next st, 3 dc in next st, hdc in next st) 4 times, sc in each st across, join with sl st in first sc (56 sts).

Continued on page 99

TECHNIQUE:
• Crochet

SIZE:
• Fits boutique-style tissue box

MATERIALS:
• Worsted-weight yarn — 2 oz. each green and red
• Tapestry needle
• G crochet hook or size needed to obtain gauge

GAUGE:
• 7 dc = 2"
• 2 dc rows = 1"

Holiday Snowman

Designed by Nancy Rigsby

STITCHING INSTRUCTIONS

1: Center and stitch design, using three strands floss for Cross Stitch and one strand floss for Backstitch.

Stitch Count:
61 wide x 89 high

Approximate Design Size:
11-count 5⅝" x 8⅛"
14-count 4⅜" x 6⅜"
16-count 3⅞" x 5⅝"
18-count 3⅜" x 5"
22-count 2⅞" x 4⅛"

Use six strands floss for Knotted Fringe Stitch (see Stitch Illustration).

2: Attach beads to front of jacket as indicated on graph. Tack jingle bells to boots as shown in photo.❄

TECHNIQUE:
• Cross Stitch

MATERIALS:
• 10" x 12" piece of smoke 14-count Aida
• Two small gold jingle bells

Knotted Fringe Stitch Illustration

Cut three strands floss into 4" lengths. Fold 4" length of floss in half; thread folded end of floss through needle forming a loop.

On right side of fabric, take a small stitch; inserting needle into fabric at #1 and out at #2. Pull needle completely through fabric leaving a loop in floss.

Insert needle through loop and pull firmly to secure stitch. Trim ends of floss to desired length when all stitches are complete.

Holiday Snowman

X	B'st	¼x	KnF	DMC	ANCHOR	J.&P. COATS	COLORS
			⊙	#304	#1003	#3410	Scarlet
				#350	#11	#3111	Coral Med.
				#699	#923	#6228	Kelly Green Dk.
				#741	#304	#2314	Tangerine Dk.
				#775	#128	#7031	Baby Blue
				#781	#309	#5309	Russet Med.
+				#783	#307	#5307	Topaz Very Dk.
				#912	#209	#6266	Seafoam Green Dk.
				#946	#332	#2332	Burnt Orange Dk.
				#963	#73	#3173	Baby Pink
	✎			#3371	#382	#5382	Darkest Brown
				White	#2	#1001	White

BEADS
◉ #02014 Black

Holiday Snowman

Holly Berry Afghan

Designed by Erma Fielder

TECHNIQUE:
• Crochet

SIZE:
• 45" x 66"

MATERIALS:
• Worsted-weight yarn — 32 oz. white, 3 oz. green and 2 oz. red
• Tapestry needle
• G and H crochet hooks or sizes needed to obtain gauges

GAUGES:
• G hook, 4 sc = 1"; 4 sc rows = 1"
• H hook, 7 sts = 2"; 4 dc rows = 2½"

AFGHAN

Row 1: With H hook and white, ch 134, dc in 4th ch from hook, (ch 4, skip next 4 chs, sc in next ch, ch 4, skip next 4 chs, 3 dc in next ch) across to last 10 chs, ch 4, skip next 4 chs, sc in next ch, ch 4, skip next 4 chs, 2 dc in last ch, turn (40 dc, 26 ch-4 sps, 13 sc).

Row 2: Ch 3, 2 dc in next st, (*ch 3, skip next ch sp, sc in next sc, ch 3, skip next ch sp, 2 dc in next st, dc in next st*, 2 dc in next st) 12 times; repeat between **, turn.

Row 3: Ch 3, dc in next st, 2 dc in next st, (*ch 2, dc in next sc, ch 2, 2 dc in next st*, dc in each of next 3 sts, 2 dc in next st) 12 times; repeat between **, dc in each of last 2 sts, turn.

Row 4: Ch 3, dc in each of next 2 sts, 2 dc in next st, (ch 1, skip next dc, 2 dc in next dc, dc in next 5 sts, 2 dc in next st) 12 times, ch 1, skip next dc, 2 dc in next dc, dc in each of last 3 sts, turn.

Row 5: Ch 1, sc in first st, (ch 4, skip next 4 sts, 3 dc in next ch-1, ch 4, skip next 4 sts, sc in next st) across, turn.

Row 6: Ch 1, sc in first st, (ch 3, 2 dc in next dc, dc in next st, 2 dc in next st, ch 3, sc in next sc) across, turn.

Row 7: Ch 5, (*2 dc in next dc, dc in each of next 3 sts, 2 dc in next st, ch 2, dc in next sc*, ch 2) 12 times; repeat between **, turn.

Row 8: Ch 4, (2 dc in next dc, dc in next 5 sts, 2 dc in next st, ch 1) 13 times, dc in 3rd ch of ch-5, turn.

Row 9: Ch 3, dc in first st, (*ch 4, skip next 4 sts, sc in next st, ch 4, skip next 4 sts*, 3 dc in next ch-1) 12 times; repeat between **, 2 dc in 3rd ch of ch-4, turn.

Rows 10-96: Repeat rows 2-9 consecutively, ending with row 8. At end of last row, **do not** turn.

Rnd 97: Working around outer edge in ends of rows and in sts, ch 1, sc in first row, [ch 4, sc in next row, (ch 4, skip next row, sc in next row) across]; working on opposite side of starting ch, ch 4, sc in first ch, ch 4, skip next 5 chs, sc in next ch, (ch 4, skip next 4 chs, sc in next ch) across, ch 4, sc in same row; repeat between [ ], ch 4, sc in first st, ch 4, skip next 4 dc, sc in next st or ch, (ch 4, skip next 4 sts, sc

in next st or ch) across to last 5 sts, ch 4, skip next 4 dc, sc in last dc, ch 4, join with sl st in first sc (152 ch sps).

Rnd 98: (Sl st, ch 1, sc) in next ch sp, ch 5, (sc, ch 5) in each ch sp around with (sc, ch 5, sc, ch 5) in each corner ch sp, join with sl st in first sc (156 ch sps).

Rnd 99: Ch 1, 4 sc in each ch sp around with 7 sc in each corner ch sp, join (108 sc between 7-sc groups on short ends, 196 sc between 7-sc groups on each long edge).

Rnd 100: Ch 1, sc in each st around with (sc, ch 2, sc) in center st of each 7-sc group, join (116 sc between corner ch sps on short ends, 204 sc between corner ch sps on long edges).

Rnds 101-105: Ch 1, sc in each st around with (sc, ch 2, sc) in each corner ch sp, join. At end of last rnd (126 sc between corner ch sps on short ends, 214 sc between corner ch sps on long edges), fasten off.

Rnd 106: Join white with sc in corner ch sp before one short end, ch 2, sc in same sp, *sc in next 21 sts, (2 sc in next st, sc in next 41 sts) 2 times, 2 sc in next st, sc in next 20 sts, (sc, ch 2, sc) in next ch sp, 2 sc in next st, sc in next 41 sts, (2 sc in next st, sc in next 42 sts) across to next corner*, (sc, ch 2, sc) in next ch sp; repeat between **, join (131 sc between corner ch sps on short ends, 221 sc between corner ch sps on long edges).

NOTES: For **picot**, ch 3, sl st in 3rd ch from hook.

For **picot shell,** (3 dc, picot, 3 dc) in next st.

Rnd 107: Sl st in next corner ch sp, (ch 3, 2 dc, picot, 3 dc) in same sp, *[sc in next st, skip next st, picot shell in next st, (skip next 2 sts, sc in next st, skip next 2 sts, picot shell in next st) across to 2 sts before next corner, skip next st, sc in next st], picot shell in next corner ch sp; repeat from * 2 more times; repeat between [ ], join with sl st in top of ch-3, fasten off.

LEAF (make 20)

Row 1: With G hook and green, ch 2, 3 sc in 2nd ch from hook, turn (3 sc).

Row 2: Ch 1, sc in each st across, turn.

Row 3: Ch 1, 2 sc in first st, sc in next st, 2 sc in last st, turn (5).

Row 4: Ch 1, 3 sc in first st, sc in each of next 3 sts, 3 sc in last st, turn (9 sc).

Row 5: Sl st in each of first 2 sts, ch 1, sc in next 5 sts leaving last 2 sts unworked, turn (5).

Row 6: Ch 1, 2 sc in first st, sc in each of next 3 sts, 2 sc in last st, turn (7).

Row 7: Ch 1, 3 sc in first st, sc in next 5 sts,

PLACEMENT DIAGRAM

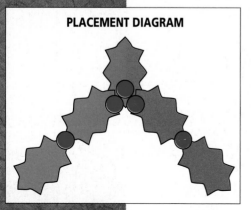

3 sc in last st, turn (11).

Row 8: Sl st in each of first 2 sts, ch 1, sc next 2 sts tog, sc next 3 sts tog, sc next 2 sts tog leaving last 2 sts unworked, turn (3).

Row 9: Ch 1, 2 sc in first st, sc in next st, 2 sc in last st, turn (5).

Row 10: Ch 1, 3 sc in first st, sc in each of next 3 sts, 3 sc in last st, turn (9).

Row 11: Sl st in each of first 2 sts, ch 1, sc next 2 sts tog, sc in next st, sc

next 2 sts tog leaving last 2 sts unworked, turn (3).

Row 12: Ch 1, sc next 3 sts tog, fasten off.

BERRY (make 20)

NOTE: Do not join rnds unless otherwise stated. Mark first st of each rnd.

Rnd 1: With G hook and red, ch 2, 6 sc in 2nd ch from hook (6 sc).

Rnd 2: 2 sc in each st around (12).

Rnds 3-4: Sc in each st around.

Rnd 5: (Sc next 2 sts tog) around, join with sl st in first sc, leaving 6" for weaving, fasten off.

Weave 6" end through sts of last rnd, pull to gather, secure end.

Sew five Leaves and five Berries to each corner of Afghan over rnds 100-107 according to Placement Diagram and as shown in photo.❈

Gilded Poinsettias Instructions on page 89

Front Assembly Diagram

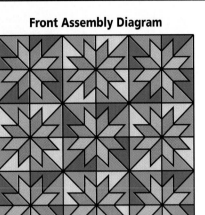

Brown Pointsettia Assembly Diagram

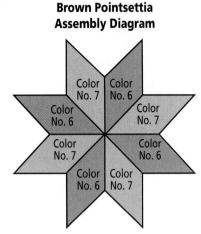

Red Poinsettia Assembly Diagram

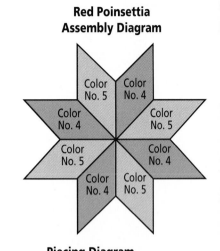

Mitering Illustration

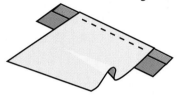

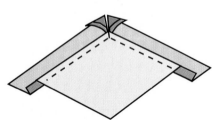

Step 1
With right sides together, sew inner border strip to edge of front piece, stopping 1/4" from each end.

Step 2
Fold border corners back at a 45 degree angle; press with right sides together. Stitch each corner along pressed line, beginning from center and working outward. Trim seam; clip corners and press open.

Piecing Diagram

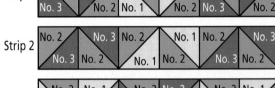

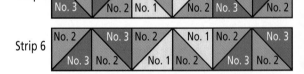

Christmas Coveralls Continued from page 91

Row 27 [29, 31]: Ch 1, hdc in each st across, turn, fasten off.

Rows 28-39 [30-39, 32-39]: Working in color sequence of red and white, repeat rows 26 and 27 [28 and 29, 30 and 31] alternately.

Row 40: Following color sequence, join next color with sl st in first st, ch 1, 2 hdc in same st, hdc in each st across with 2 hdc in last st, turn (30) [31, 35].

Rows 41-42 [41-46, 41-50]: Repeat rows 27 and 40 [29 and 40, 31 and 40] alternately, ending with (32) [37, 45] sts in last row.

Row 43 [47, 51]: Sl st in each of first 2 [2, 3] sts, ch 1, hdc last worked st and next st tog, hdc in each st across to last 3 [3, 4] sts, hdc next 2 sts tog leaving last sts unworked, turn, fasten off (28) [33, 39].

Row 44 [48, 52]: Following color sequence, join next color with sl st in first st, ch 1, hdc same st and next st tog, hdc in each st across to last 2 sts, hdc last 2 sts tog, turn (26) [31, 37].

Row 45 [49, 53]: Ch 1, hdc first 2sts tog, hdc in each st across to last 2 sts, hdc last 2 sts tog, turn, fasten off (24) [29, 37].

Rows 46-47 [50-53, 54-57]: Repeat rows 44 and 45 [48 and 49, 52 and 53] alternately, ending with 20 [21, 29] sts in last row.

Matching center of Sleeve to shoulder seam, with white, sew Sleeves to armholes. With white for Sleeve and green for body, sew Sleeve and side seams.✿

98

Pretty Presentation Continued from page 93

Rnd 5: Ch 1, sc in each st around with 3 sc in center st of each 3-dc group, join (64 sc).

Rnd 6: Working this rnd in **back lps** only, ch 3, dc in each st around, join with sl st in top of ch-3.

Rnds 7-16: Ch 3, dc in each st around, join.

Rnd 17: Ch 1, sc in each st around, join with sl st in first sc, fasten off.

RIBBON (make 4)

Row 1: With red, ch 6, sc in 2nd ch from hook, sc in each ch across, turn (5 sc).

Rows 2-31: Ch 1, sc in each st across, turn. At end of last row, fasten off.

BOW LOOP (make 4)

Row 1: Repeat same row of Ribbon.

Rows 2-20: Ch 1, sc in each st across, turn.

Row 21: Hold rows 1 and 20 together, matching sts; working through both thicknesses, ch 1, sc in each st across, fasten off.

FINISHING

1: Sew one Ribbon centered to each side of Cover as shown in photo.

2: With row 1 to outside, sew one Bow Loop to top end of each Ribbon.

3: Cut 12" strand of red. With tapestry needle, weave strand through row 18 of each Bow Loop, pull ends of strand to make Bow Loops stand up, secure ends.❈

Candy Bucket Instructions on page 92

ribbons to side as shown in photo. Thread wire through side and han- dle according to Handle Attachment Diagram.❈

CANDY BUCKET COLOR KEY:

	Worsted- weight	Nylon Plus™	Need- loft®	Yarn Amount
☐ White	#01	#41	20 yds.
■ Red	#19	#02	14 yds.
■ Green	#58	#28	12 yds.
■ Cinnamon	#44	#14	1½ yds.

C – Handle
(cut 1) 13 x 17 holes
Lap Under

Lap Over

D – Handle End
(cut 2) 3 x 3 holes

B – Bottom (cut 1) 27 x 27 holes

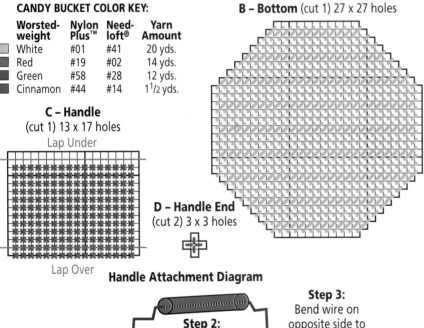

A – Side (cut 1) 27 x 90 holes

Lap Under

Lap Over

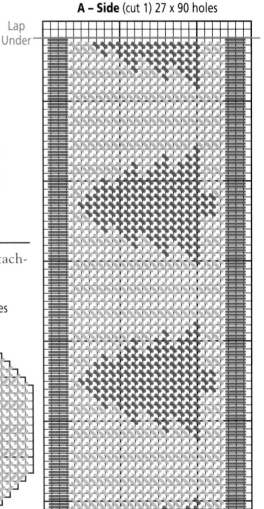

Handle Attachment Diagram

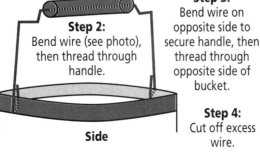

Step 1:
Hook one end of wire from outside to inside through top edge of side; bend to secure.

Step 2:
Bend wire (see photo), then thread through handle.

Step 3:
Bend wire on opposite side to secure handle, then thread through opposite side of bucket.

Step 4:
Cut off excess wire.

Side

Joy to the World

Uplifting designs with a religious theme help us keep the true meaning of the Christmas season in mind. Pay homage to the King with majestic needlework pieces in cross stitch and plastic canvas that depict His humble beginning and His joyous triumph. Spread His love by giving hand-crafted gifts that extol the virtues of a loving heart and a meek, gentle spirit.

Blessed Nativity

Nativity Tissue Cover
instructions on page 112

Nativity Holder
instructions on page 105

*Nativity Wreath
instructions on page 104*

Nativity Coasters instructions on page 113

Nativity Wreath

Designed by Mary K. Perry

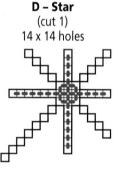

TECHNIQUE:
• Plastic Canvas

SIZE:
• Insert fits inside a wreath with a 6½-7" opening

MATERIALS:
• One sheet of 7-count plastic canvas
• Grapevine wreath with a 6½-7" opening
• Floral wire and/or craft glue or glue gun
• #3 pearl cotton or six-strand embroidery floss (for amount see Color Key)
• ⅛" metallic ribbon or metallic cord (for amounts see Color Key)
• Worsted-weight or plastic canvas yarn (for amounts see Color Key)

CUTTING INSTRUCTIONS

NOTE: Photo on page 103.

A: For insert, cut one according to graph.

B: For shepherd, cut one according to graph.

C: For lamb, cut one according to graph.

D: For star, cut one according to graph.

NATIVITY WREATH COLOR KEY:

#3 pearl cotton or floss			Amount
■ Black			7 yds.

Metallic ribbon or cord			Amount
▨ Gold			3 yds.

Worsted-weight	Nylon Plus™	Need-loft®	Yarn Amount
□ Beige	#43	#40	13 yds.
▨ Cinnamon	#44	#14	10 yds.
▨ White	#01	#41	6 yds.
▨ Maple	#35	#13	5 yds.
▨ Gray	#23	#38	3 yds.
▨ Crimson	#53	#42	2 yds.
▨ Dk. Rust	#16	#10	2 yds.
▨ Eggshell	#24	#39	2 yds.
▨ Royal	#09	#32	2 yds.
▨ Navy	#45	#31	1½ yds.
■ Black	#02	#00	1 yd.
▨ Peach	#46	#47	1 yd.
▨ Sail Blue	#04	#35	1 yd.

STITCH KEY:
— Backstitch/Straight Stitch
• French Knot

STITCHING INSTRUCTIONS

1: Using colors and stitches indicated, work A-D pieces according to graphs; fill in uncoded areas of A using beige and Continental Stitch. With black for lamb hooves, tail and muzzle and gray for shepherd's staff as shown in photo and with matching colors, Overcast unfinished edges of A-D pieces.

2: Using colors indicated (use pearl cotton or six strands floss for outlines), Backstitch, Straight Stitch and French Knot, embroider detail indicated on A graph. Using yarn colors indicated, Straight Stitch and French Knot, embroider detail as indicated on B and C graphs.

3: Wire or glue motifs to wreath as shown.✻

C – Lamb
(cut 1)
12 x 13 holes

D – Star
(cut 1)
14 x 14 holes

A – Insert
(cut 1) 44 x 47 holes

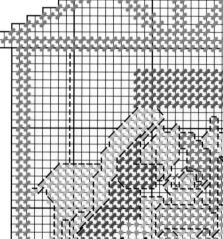

B – Shepherd
(cut 1)
10 x 24 holes

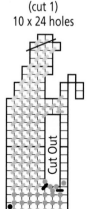

Cut Out

Nativity Holder

Designed by Mary K. Perry

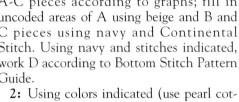

CUTTING INSTRUCTIONS

NOTES: Photo on page 102. Graphs continued on page 114.

A: For front, cut one according to graph.

B: For back, cut one 29 x 51 holes.

C: For end #1 and #2, cut one each 21 x 29 holes.

D: For bottom, cut one 21 x 51 holes (no graph).

STITCHING INSTRUCTIONS

1: Using yarn and metallic ribbon or cord in colors and stitches indicated, work A-C pieces according to graphs; fill in uncoded areas of A using beige and B and C pieces using navy and Continental Stitch. Using navy and stitches indicated, work D according to Bottom Stitch Pattern Guide.

2: Using colors indicated (use pearl cotton or six strands floss for outlines), Backstitch and Straight Stitch, embroider detail as indicated on graphs.

3: With matching colors as shown in photo, Whipstitch A-D pieces together; Overcast unfinished edges. ❋

Graphs continued on page 114.

TECHNIQUE:
• Plastic Canvas

SIZE:
• 3¼" x 7⅞" x 7¼" tall

MATERIALS:
• 1½ sheets of 7-count plastic canvas
• #3 pearl cotton or six-strand embroidery floss (for amount see Color Key)
• ⅛" metallic ribbon or metallic cord (for amounts see Color Key)
• Worsted-weight or plastic canvas yarn (for amounts see Color Key)

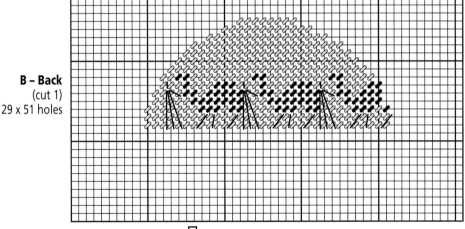

B – Back
(cut 1)
29 x 51 holes

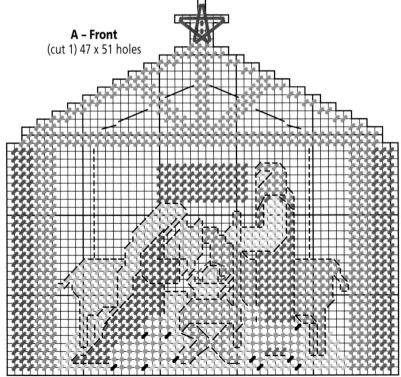

A – Front
(cut 1) 47 x 51 holes

NATIVITY HOLDER COLOR KEY:

#3 pearl cotton or floss			Amount
■ Black			8 yds.

Metallic ribbon or cord			Amount
■ Gold			4 yds.
▨ Pearl/White			3 yds.

Worsted-weight	Nylon Plus™	Need-loft®	Yarn Amount
■ Navy	#45	#31	2 oz.
□ Beige	#43	#40	11 yds.
▨ Cinnamon	#44	#14	10 yds.
□ White	#01	#41	8 yds.
▨ Yellow	#26	#57	6 yds.
▨ Maple	#35	#13	5 yds.
■ Black	#02	#00	3 yds.
▨ Crimson	#53	#42	2 yds.
▨ Dk. Rust	#16	#10	2 yds.
▨ Gray	#23	#38	2 yds.
▨ Royal	#09	#32	2 yds.
▨ Eggshell	#24	#39	1 yd.
▨ Peach	#46	#47	1 yd.
▨ Sail Blue	#04	#35	1 yd.

STITCH KEY:
— Backstitch/Straight Stitch

Joyous Sentiments

Designed by Jacquelyn Fox

TECHNIQUE:
• Cross Stitch

MATERIALS:
• 9" x 13" piece of blush 14-count Aida
• Fingertip towel with 14-count Aida design area
• Wooden box with 4" x 10" design area

STITCHING INSTRUCTIONS
NOTE: Graph on page 115.
1: Center and stitch design onto Aida and Fingertip® towel, using two strands floss or one strand floss held together with one strand blending filament (as indicated) for Cross Stitch and Backstitch of beaks. Use one strand floss for remaining Backstitch and French Knots. Cover design area of box with Aida, following manufacturer's instructions.✿

Daily Devotional

Designed by Lisa Edelbach

STITCHING INSTRUCTIONS

NOTES: All seams are ½" unless otherwise noted. Graph on page 115.

1: Center and stitch design on right side of Aida, using two strands floss for Cross Stitch and three strands floss for Backstitch.

2: Trim stitched Aida ¾" larger than design. From fabric, cut one piece 15⅝" wide x 10⅝" tall for bible covering, two pieces 5" wide x 10⅝" tall for inside flaps, and two 3" x 10⅝" pieces for handles. Center and stitch Aida to right side of bible covering 1½" from short edge. Weave metallic ribbon through ½" lace along straight edge as shown in photo. Stitch to outside edge of stitched Aida.

3: For handles, with right sides together, fold each 3" x 10⅝" piece in half lengthwise; stitch together along long edges. Trim seams and turn right side out. Finish one long edge of each flap. With right sides together, stitch unfinished edges of flaps to front, positioning one handle evenly between covering and flaps on each side. Trim seams and clip curves. Turn flaps to inside; press. Turn top and bottom edges to inside; press. Finish edges; slip stitch in place.❄

TECHNIQUE:
- Cross Stitch & Sewing

SIZE:
- Fits 1⅜" x 6⅝" x 9⅝" bible

MATERIALS:
- 9" x 10" piece of 14-count ivory Aida
- ½ yd. fabric
- 1 yd. metallic ½" beading lace
- 1 yd metallic ⅛" ribbon
- Thread

THY WORD IS A
LAMP TO MY FEET
AND A LIGHT
TO MY PATH

Sacred Words

Designed by Lois Winston

CUTTING INSTRUCTIONS

A: For front and back, use two (one for front and one for back) 70- x 90-hole sheets.

B: For ends, cut two 22 x 70 holes (no graph).

C: For bottom, cut one 22 x 90 holes (no graph).

D: For handles, cut two 6 x 90 holes (no graph).

STITCHING INSTRUCTIONS

1: Using colors indicated and Continental Stitch, work one A for front according to graph; fill in uncoded areas

Continued on page 115

SACRED WORDS COLOR KEY:

Metallic braid or cord			Amount
Gold			8 yds.
Silver			6 yds.

Worsted-weight	Nylon Plus™	Need-loft®	Yarn Amount
Black	#02	#00	6 oz.
Lavender	#22	#45	16 yds.
Eggshell	#24	#39	15 yds.
Camel	#34	#43	6 yds.
Sail Blue	#04	#35	5 yds.
Pink	#11	#07	4 yds.
Purple	#21	#46	4 yds.
Mint	#30	#24	2 yds.
Beige	#43	#40	1 yd.

STITCH KEY:

— Backstitch/Straight Stitch

TECHNIQUE:
• Plastic Canvas

SIZE:
• 3½" x 13⅝" x 10⅝" tall, not including handles

MATERIALS:
• Four sheets of 7-count plastic canvas
• Heavy metallic braid or metallic cord (for amounts see Color Key)
• Worsted-weight or plastic canvas yarn (for amounts see Color Key)

Handle Attachment   Handle Attachment

A – Front (use one 70- x 90-hole sheet)

Peaceful Hearts

Designed by Jacquelyn Fox

TECHNIQUE:
• Cross Stitch

MATERIALS:
• 8" x 12" piece of light oatmeal Fiddler's Lite®
• Wooden tray with 10" square design area

STITCHING INSTRUCTIONS

NOTE: Double mats were professionally cut at a local frame shop.

1: Center and stitch design, using two strands floss for Cross Stitch, Backstitch of bushes, bird's beak and French Knots of eyes. Use one strand floss for remaining Backstitch and French Knots.

2: Position and secure stitched Fiddler's Lite® in tray opening following manufacturer's instructions.❖

Stitch Count:
104 wide x 137 high

Approximate Design Size:
11-count 9½" x 12½"
14-count 7½" x 9⅞"
16-count 6½" x 8⅝"
18-count 5⅞" x 7⅝"
22-count 4¾" x 6¼"

X	B'st	¹/₄x	Fr	DMC	ANCHOR	J.&P. COATS	COLORS
■	◩			#318	#399	#8511	Silver Med.
■	◩			#347	#1025	#3013	Rose Coral Dk.
			◉	#355	#1014	#2339	Terra Cotta Very Dk.
◉	◩			#640	#903	#5393	Beige Grey Very Dk.
■	◩			#644	#830	#5830	Beige Grey Lt.
	◩	◩		#676	#891	#2305	Honey
	◩			#801	#359	#5472	Coffee Brown Dk.
	◩		◉	#3371	#382	#5382	Darkest Brown
■	◩			#3712	#1023	#3071	Salmon Med.
▧	◩			#3779	#868	#3868	Terra Cotta Very Lt.
■	◩			#3790	#393	#5393	Beige Grey Dk.
⊤	◩			White	#2	#1001	White

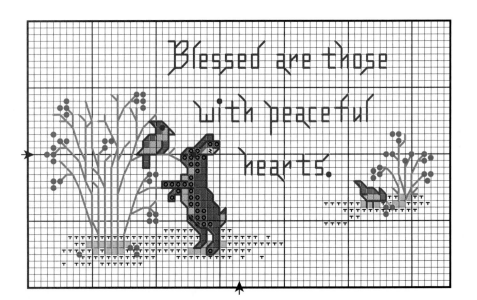

110

Nativity Tissue Cover

Designed by Mary K. Perry

CUTTING INSTRUCTIONS
NOTE: Photo on page 102. Graphs continued on page 114.

A: For top, cut one according to graph.
B: For sides, cut four 29 x 37 holes.

STITCHING INSTRUCTIONS

1: Using colors and stitches indicated, work A according to graph; work one B piece according to each graph. Fill in uncoded areas using navy and Continental Stitch; Overcast unfinished cutout edges of top.

2: Using colors indicated, (use pearl cotton or six strands floss for outlines) Backstitch and Straight Stitch, embroider detail as indicated on graphs.

3: Positioning one angel side on each

Continued on page 114

B – Side #1 (cut 1) 29 x 37 holes

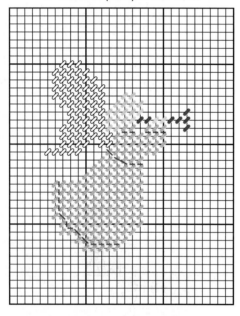

A – Top (cut 1) 29 x 29 holes

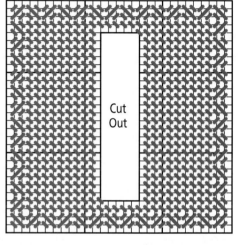

Cut Out

B – Side #2 (cut 1) 29 x 37 holes

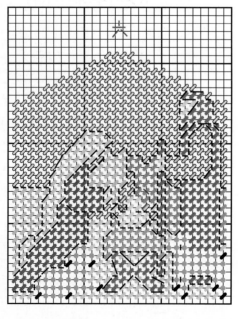

NATIVITY TISSUE COVER COLOR KEY:

#3 pearl cotton or floss			Amount
■ Black			6 yds.

Metallic ribbon or cord			Amount
■ Gold			4 yds.
▨ Pearl/White			3 yds.

Worsted-weight	Nylon Plus™	Need-loft®	Yarn Amount
■ Navy	#45	#31	3 oz.
▨ Beige	#43	#40	7 yds.
■ White	#01	#41	7 yds.
■ Maple	#35	#13	6 yds.
■ Cinnamon	#44	#14	3 yds.
■ Crimson	#53	#42	2 yds.
■ Dk. Rust	#16	#10	2 yds.
■ Gray	#23	#38	2 yds.
■ Royal	#09	#32	2 yds.
■ Peach	#46	#47	1½ yds.
■ Sail Blue	#04	#35	1½ yds.
▨ Lt. Green	#28	#26	1 yd.
■ Black	#02	#00	1 yd.

STITCH KEY:

— Backstitch/Straight Stitch

Nativity Coasters

Designed by Mary K. Perry

CUTTING INSTRUCTIONS

NOTE: Photo on page 103.

A: For Coaster fronts and backs, cut eight (four for fronts and four for backs) 24 x 24 holes.

B: For Holder front, cut one according to graph.

C: For Holder back, cut one 16 x 28 holes (no graph).

D: For Holder ends, cut two 10 x 16 holes (no graph).

E: For Holder bottom, cut one 10 x 28 holes (no graph).

STITCHING INSTRUCTIONS

1: Using colors and stitches indicated, work A (four for fronts and four for backs) and B pieces according to graphs; fill in uncoded areas using navy and Continental Stitch. Using navy and stitches indicated, work C-E pieces according to Coaster Holder Stitch Pattern Guide.

2: Using colors indicated, Backstitch, Straight Stitch and Smyrna Cross Stitch, embroider detail as indicated on graphs.

3: For each Coaster, holding one of each A wrong sides together, with navy, Whipstitch together. For Holder, Whipstitch B-E pieces together. With matching colors as shown in photo, Overcast unfinished edges.❀

TECHNIQUE:
• Plastic Canvas

SIZE:
• Each Coaster is 3¾" square
• Holder is 1⅝" x 4⅜" x 4½" tall

MATERIALS:
• 1½ sheets of 7-count plastic canvas
• ⅛" metallic ribbon or metallic cord (for amounts see Color Key)
• Worsted-weight or plastic canvas yarn (for amounts see Color Key)

NATIVITY COASTERS COLOR KEY:

Metallic ribbon or cord			Amount
Gold			7 yds.
Pearl/White			3 yds.

Worsted-weight	Nylon Plus™	Need-loft®	Yarn Amount
Navy	#45	#31	2 oz.
Maple	#35	#13	10 yds.
White	#01	#41	7 yds.
Eggshell	#24	#39	4 yds.
Gray	#23	#38	3 yds.
Black	#02	#00	2 yds.
Beige	#43	#40	1 yd.
Peach	#46	#47	½ yd.
Crimson	#53	#42	¼ yd.
Royal	#09	#32	¼ yd.
Sail Blue	#04	#35	¼ yd.

STITCH KEY:

- — Backstitch/Straight Stitch
- ✳ Smyrna Cross Stitch

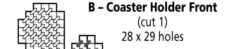
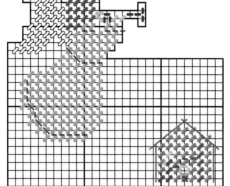

B – Coaster Holder Front
(cut 1)
28 x 29 holes

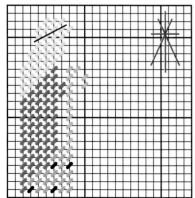

A – Coaster Front (cut 4) 24 x 24 holes

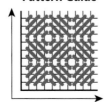

Coaster Holder Stitch Pattern Guide

Continue established pattern up and across each entire piece.

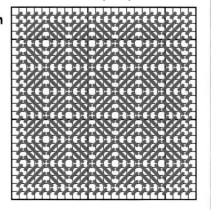

A – Coaster Back (cut 4) 24 x 24 holes

Nativity Tissue Cover

Continued from page 112

side of manger scene, with navy, Whipstitch A and B pieces together; Overcast unfinished edges.❅

#3 pearl cotton or floss			Amount
■ Black			6 yds.

Metallic ribbon or cord			Amount
■ Gold			4 yds.
▨ Pearl/White			3 yds.

Worsted-weight	Nylon Plus™	Need-loft®	Yarn Amount
■ Navy	#45	#31	3 oz.
▨ Beige	#43	#40	7 yds.
■ White	#01	#41	7 yds.
■ Maple	#35	#13	6 yds.
■ Cinnamon	#44	#14	3 yds.

NATIVITY TISSUE COVER COLOR KEY:

Worsted-weight	Nylon Plus™	Need-loft®	Yarn Amount
■ Crimson	#53	#42	2 yds.
■ Dk. Rust	#16	#10	2 yds.
■ Gray	#23	#38	2 yds.
■ Royal	#09	#32	2 yds.
■ Peach	#46	#47	1½ yds.
■ Sail Blue	#04	#35	1½ yds.
▨ Lt. Green	#28	#26	1 yd.
■ Black	#02	#00	1 yd.

STITCH KEY:
— Backstitch/Straight Stitch

B – Side #4
(cut 1)
29 x 37 holes

B – Side #3
(cut 1)
29 x 37 holes

Nativity Holder Instructions on page 105

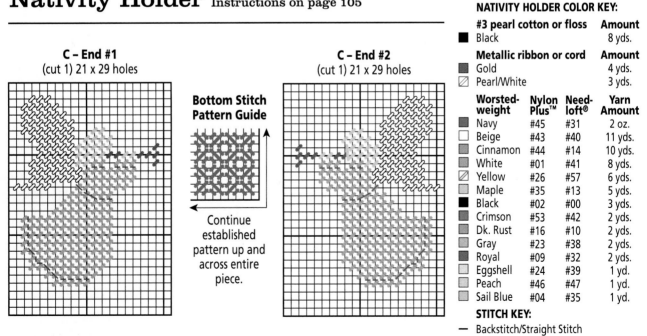

C – End #1
(cut 1) 21 x 29 holes

Bottom Stitch Pattern Guide

Continue established pattern up and across entire piece.

C – End #2
(cut 1) 21 x 29 holes

NATIVITY HOLDER COLOR KEY:

#3 pearl cotton or floss			Amount
■ Black			8 yds.

Metallic ribbon or cord			Amount
■ Gold			4 yds.
▨ Pearl/White			3 yds.

Worsted-weight	Nylon Plus™	Need-loft®	Yarn Amount
■ Navy	#45	#31	2 oz.
□ Beige	#43	#40	11 yds.
■ Cinnamon	#44	#14	10 yds.
■ White	#01	#41	8 yds.
▨ Yellow	#26	#57	6 yds.
■ Maple	#35	#13	5 yds.
■ Black	#02	#00	3 yds.
■ Crimson	#53	#42	2 yds.
■ Dk. Rust	#16	#10	2 yds.
■ Gray	#23	#38	2 yds.
■ Royal	#09	#32	2 yds.
■ Eggshell	#24	#39	1 yd.
■ Peach	#46	#47	1 yd.
■ Sail Blue	#04	#35	1 yd.

STITCH KEY:
— Backstitch/Straight Stitch

Joyous Sentiments Instructions on page 106

Stitch Count:
89 wide x 21 high

Approximate Design Size:
11-count 8⅛" x 2"
14-count 6⅜" x 1½"
16-count 5⅝" x 1⅜"
18-count 5" x 1¼"
22-count 4⅛" x 1"

X	B'st	¼x	Fr	DMC	ANCHOR	J.&P. COATS	KREINIK (BF)	COLORS
▨			◪	#352	#9	#3008		Peach Flesh Dk.
	▨	◪		#433	#358	#5471		Coffee Brown
▨		◪		#436	#1045	#5943		Toast
▨				#502	#877	#6876		Sage Green Med. held together with
							#043	Confetti Green
＋				#754	#1012	#2331		Peach Flesh Lt.
▨		◪		#840	#379	#5379		Pecan Med.
	▨		●	#3371	#382	#5382		Darkest Brown

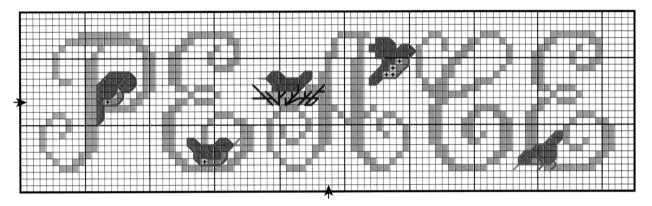

Daily Devotional Instructions on page 107

Stitch Count:
39 wide x 59 high

Approximate Design Size:
11-count 3⅝" x 5⅜"
14-count 2⅞" x 4¼"
16-count 2½" x 3¾"
18-count 2¼" x 3⅜"
22-count 1⅞" x 2¾"

X	B'st	¼x	DMC	ANCHOR	J.&P. COATS	COLORS
■		◪	#550	#102	#4107	Darkest Amethyst
	▨		#280			Gold Metallic

Sacred Words
Continued from page 109

and work remaining A and B-D pieces using black and Continental Stitch. Using gold metallic braid or metallic cord and Straight Stitch, embroider detail on crosses as indicated on graph.

2: With eggshell, Overcast unfinished long edges of D pieces. Whipstitch A-C pieces together, catching short ends of handles on front and back as indicated to join as you work.❀

Silver and Gold

Dress your home in true holiday style
with glistening, gilded accents that
sparkle and shine. Radiating a
subtle richness all their own, these
opulent examples of needlecraft's
treasures will enhance your decor
with priceless beauty. From modern,
stylized sun and star motifs to
traditional toy soldiers, these
superb creations will become an
invaluable part of your holiday decor.

Celestial Accents

Designed by Fran Rohus

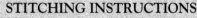

TECHNIQUE:
• Plastic Canvas

SIZE:
• Sun Ornament is 7¾" x 7¾"
• Star Ornament is 4¼" x 5"
• Star Wreath is 12" across
• Trinket Box is 3¾" tall x 7¾" across

MATERIALS:
• Three sheets of 7-count plastic canvas
• 12" pine wreath
• 3 yds. blue ⅜" satin ribbon
• 5 yds. white/gold metallic stripe 6"-wide tulle
• Two 9" x 12" sheets of dk. blue felt
• Gold star garland
• Six 18" lengths of 18-gauge floral wire
• Monofilament fishing line
• Craft glue or glue gun
• Metallic cord (for amounts see Color Key on page 126)
• Worsted-weight or plastic canvas yarn (for amount see Color Key)

CUTTING INSTRUCTIONS

NOTE: Graphs and illustrations on pages 126 and 127.

A: For Sun rays, cut two according to graph.

B: For Sun center, cut two according to graph.

C: For Star frame, cut two according to graph.

D: For Star center, cut two according to graph.

E: For Wreath stars, cut eight according to graph.

F: For Trinket Box lid top, cut one according to graph.

G: For Tinket Box lid side pieces, cut two 3 x 83 holes (no graph).

H: For Trinket Box side, cut two 22 x 78 holes (no graph).

I: For Trinket Box bottom, cut one according to graph.

J: For Trinket Box lining side and bottom pieces, cut pieces from felt according to Felt Cutting Illustration.

STITCHING INSTRUCTIONS

NOTE: I piece is unworked.

1: For Ornaments, using gold for Sun rays and Star frame, silver for Sun and Star centers and Continental Stitch, work A-D pieces. Holding matching pieces wrong sides together, with matching colors, Whipstitch together. Tie pieces together with fishing line as shown in photo.

2: For Wreath, using gold and Long Stitch, work E pieces according to graph; Overcast unfinished edges. Using silver and Straight Stitch, embroider outlines as indicated on graph.

NOTES: Cut one 3-yd. length each of gold and silver. Cut tulle into one 1-yd. and two 2-yd. lengths; set 1-yd. length aside for Trinket Box.

3: Holding 3-yd. strands of gold and silver together with ribbon, wrap around pine wreath as shown; glue to secure. Holding one 2-yd. length of tulle at back of wreath, push a tuft through branches every

Continued on page 126

118

119

Snowfall Table Set

Designed by Nancy Marshall

STITCHING INSTRUCTIONS

1: Stitch "Place Mat" design on each short end of 13" x 18" piece of Valerie, "Bread Cover" design on each corner of 18" x 18" piece of Valerie, starting 1" from outside edges, and "Napkin Ring" design onto 3" x 3" piece of Valerie, stitching over two threads and using three strands floss for Cross Stitch and two strands floss or thread for Backstitch.

2: To fray ends on place mat and bread cover, stay stitch ½" from edges; pull out threads.

3: For napkin ring, with right sides together, sew stitched Valerie to backing fabric, stitching close to design and leaving an opening; trim seam. Turn right side out and slip stitch opening closed; press. Center and glue ¼"-wide ribbon on ⅝"-wide ribbon. Center and glue this unit on ⅞"-wide ribbon as shown in photo. Stitch ribbon ends together, forming ring. Tack stitched design to ribbon.❄

Bread Cover
Stitch Count:
46 wide x 46 high

Approximate Design Size:
11-count 4⅛" x 4⅛"
14-count 3⅜" x 3⅜"
16-count 2⅞" x 2⅞"
18-count 2⅝" x 2⅝"
22-count 2⅛" x 2⅛"
20-count over two
  threads 4⅝" x 4⅝"

TECHNIQUE:
• Cross Stitch

MATERIALS:
• One 3" x 3" piece, one 13" x 18" piece and one 18" x 18" piece of 20-count silver/white Valerie
• 3" x 3" piece of backing fabric
• 6" piece each of ⅞", ⅝" and ¼"-wide grosgrain ribbon
• Craft glue

Napkin Ring
Stitch Count:
18 wide x 18 high

Approximate Design Size:
11-count 1⅝" x 1⅝"
14-count 1⅜" x 1⅜"
16-count 1⅛" x 1⅛"
18-count 1" x 1"
22-count ⅞" x ⅞"
20-count over two
  threads 1⅞" x 1⅞"

Place Mat
Stitch Count:
108 wide x 20 high

Approximate Design Size:
11-count 9⅞" x 1⅞"
14-count 7¾" x 1½"
16-count 6¾" x 1¼"
18-count 6" x 1⅛"
22-count 5" x 1"
20-count over two
  threads 10⅞" x 2"

Bread Cover

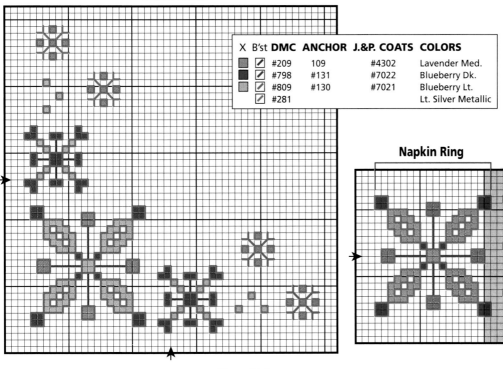

X	B'st	DMC	ANCHOR	J.&P. COATS	COLORS
	✎	#209	109	#4302	Lavender Med.
	✎	#798	#131	#7022	Blueberry Dk.
	✎	#809	#130	#7021	Blueberry Lt.
	✎	#281			Lt. Silver Metallic

Napkin Ring

Place Mat

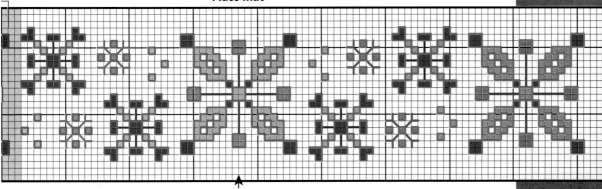

Toy Soldier Quartet

Designed by Vicki Blizzard

TECHNIQUE:
• Plastic Canvas

SIZE:
• Large Soldier is 8⅜" tall
• Medium Soldier is 6¼" tall
• Small Soldier is 4⅛" tall
• Tiny Soldier is 3" tall

MATERIALS FOR ONE OF EACH:
• ½ sheet each of 5-count and 7-count plastic canvas
• ¼ sheet each of 10-count and 14-count plastic canvas
• Six gold 3-mm, 5-mm and 8-mm beads
• Six gold ¼" jingle bells
• Sewing needle and gold metallic thread
• Craft glue or glue gun
• Metallic cord, heavy metallic braid or metallic cord, medium and fine metallic braid (for amounts see Color Key)
• Six-strand embroidery floss (for amounts see Color Key)
• #3 pearl cotton or 12 strands floss (for amounts see Color Key)
• Worsted-weight or plastic canvas yarn (for amounts see Color Key)

CUTTING INSTRUCTIONS

NOTE: Use 5-count for Large, 7-count for Medium, 10-count for Small and 14-count for Tiny Soldier.

A: For sides, cut one from each size canvas 33 x 40 holes (no graph).

B: For tops and bottoms, cut two (one for top and one for bottom) from each size canvas according to graph.

C: For arms, cut two from each size canvas according to graph.

D: For feathers, cut one from each size canvas according to graph.

STITCHING INSTRUCTIONS

NOTE: Use a doubled strand of yarn and metallic cord for Large, a single strand of yarn and cord or heavy metallic braid for Medium, pearl cotton or 12 strands floss and medium metallic braid for Small and six strands floss and fine metallic braid for Tiny Soldier.

1: Centering motif and omitting one row of stitches at each short end of each piece, using colors indicated (see photo for hat/belt/boot, jacket/sleeve and pants colors) and Continental Stitch, work A pieces according to Toy Soldier Body Motif Graph.

2: Using colors indicated (use a single strand of yarn for Large, pearl cotton or 12 strands floss for eyes and mouth for Medium, six strands floss for eyes and mouth for Small and three strands floss for Tiny Soldier), French

Continued on page 127

B – Top & Bottom
(cut 1 each from each size canvas)
10 x 10 holes

Toy Soldier Body Motif Graph

D – Feather
(cut 1 from each size canvas)
3 x 6 holes

C – Arm
(cut 2 from each size canvas)
5 x 14 holes

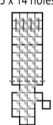

← →
Continue established background pattern across each entire piece.

Decorating Ideas

To make the large soldier into a doorstop, fill the body before closing with a weight such as small stones or Poly Pellets®.

To add a hanger, before Whipstitching top to body, secure ends of a loop of metallic cord or braid to top. Medium soldier may be used as a door hanger, small soldier as a tree ornament and tiny soldier as a package topper.

For optional hand-held bells, tie one ½" gold bell to each end of one strand of metallic cord or braid. Glue center of each strand to body under hand (see medium soldier photo).

TOY SOLDIERS COLOR KEY:			LARGE	MEDIUM	SMALL	TINY
Metallic			**Cord**	**Hvy.Braid**	**Med.Braid**	**FineBraid**
■ Dk. Red			6 yds.	5½ yds.	4 yds.	3 yds.
Worsted-weight	**Nylon Plus™**	**Need-loft®**	**Yarn Amount**	**Yarn Amount**	**PearlCotton Amount**	**Floss Amount**
■ Black	#02	#00	34 yds.	6 yds.	15 yds.	5 yds.
☐ Royal	#09	#32	12 yds.	6 yds.	7 yds.	10 yds.
☐ White	#01	#41	14 yds.	15 yds.	8 yds.	5 yds.
☐ Flesh	#14	#56	2 yds.	1 yd.	1 yd.	½ yd.
☐ Silver	#40	#37	2 yds.	1 yd.	1 yd.	1 yd.
☐ Pink	#11	#07	1 yd.	½ yd.	½ yd.	½ yd.
■ Dk. Red	#20	#01	½ yd.	¼ yd.	¼ yd.	¼ yd.
■ Hat/Belt/Boot Color						
☐ Jacket/Sleeve Color						
■ Pants Color						

STITCH KEY:
— Backstitch/Straight Stitch
• French Knot
▲ Bead/Bell Attachment

TECHNIQUE:
• Plastic Canvas

SIZE:
• 7¼" long (monogram hangs over top of book)

MATERIALS FOR ONE:
• Scraps of colored 7- and clear 10-count plastic canvas
• 12-15 seed beads (optional)
• Craft glue or glue gun
• Medium metallic braid or six-strand embroidery floss (for amounts see Color Key on page 129)
• #3 pearl cotton and/or heavy metallic braid (for amounts see Color Key)

Monogram Bookmarks

Designed by Vicki Blizzard

CUTTING INSTRUCTIONS
NOTE: Graphs on pages 128 and 129.

A: For initial, cut letter of choice from 10-count according to graph.

B: For bookmark, cut one from colored 7-count according to graph.

C: For bookmark brace, cut one from colored 7-count 2 x 4 holes (no graph).

STITCHING INSTRUCTIONS
NOTE: B and C pieces are unworked.

1: Using #3 pearl cotton or heavy metallic braid and Continental Stitch, work A; Overcast unfinished edges.

2: For flowered initial, using medium braid or six strands floss, Backstitch, Straight Stitch and French Knot (**NOTE:** If desired, with two strands matching color floss, sew beads to A in place of French Knots), embroider as indicated on graph. For striped initial, omit leaves and French Knot or bead flowers.

3: Glue A-C pieces together according to Bookmark Assembly Diagram.❀

Night Jewels Ornaments

Designed by Jocelyn Sass

STAR
SIDE (make 2)

NOTE: Do not join rnds unless otherwise stated. Mark first st of each rnd.

Rnd 1: With cord, ch 2, 6 sc in 2nd ch from hook (6 sc).

Rnd 2: 2 sc in each st around (12).

Rnd 3: (Sc in next st, 2 sc in next st) around (18 sc).

Rnd 4: (Sc in each of next 2 sts, 2 sc in next st) 5 times, sc in each of next 2 sts, 3 sc in last st (25 sc).

Rnd 5: *Sl st in each of next 2 sts, 2 hdc
Continued on page 129

TECHNIQUE:
• Crochet

SIZE:
• Star is 3⅜" across
• Heart is 2¾" x 3½"
• Wreath is 3½" across

MATERIALS FOR ALL THREE:
• Metallic cord — 52 yds. multi-black
• Black worsted-weight yarn (for stuffing)
• 9" each yellow, pink and blue ¼" ribbon
• One each yellow, pink and blue 18-mm ribbon roses
• Craft glue or hot glue gun
• G crochet hook or size needed to obtain gauge

GAUGE:
• 4 sc sts = 1"
• 4 sc rows or rnds = 1"

Celestial Accents Continued from page 118

few inches (see photo); tie remaining 2-yd. length into a double loop bow.

NOTES: Cut six 18" lengths of silver cord; remove white core from strands. Thread one wire into each hollow strand of cord; wrap around pencil to form spirals.

4: Glue star garland, silver spirals and bow to bottom of wreath. Glue one E to bow and remaining E pieces to wreath as shown.

5: For Trinket Box, using colors indicated and Long Stitch, work F according to graph. Overlapping

three holes at ends and working through both thicknesses at overlap areas to join, work G pieces according to Trinket Box Lid Side Stitch Pattern Guide. Overlapping three holes at ends as for lid side, work H pieces according to Trinket Box Side Stitch Pattern Guide.

6: With royal, Whipstitch F and lid side together, forming lid;

Whipstitch box side and I together, forming box. Overcast unfinished edges of lid and box.

NOTE: Cut 1-yd length of tulle in half.

7: Glue one end of each tulle to inside on opposite edges of lid side. Tie ends into a single or double loop bow; glue bow to lid to secure. Glue J pieces inside box.❄

CELESTIAL ACCENTS COLOR KEY:

Metallic cord			Amount
☐ Gold			58 yds.
■ Silver			21 yds.

Worsted-weight	Nylon Plus™	Need-loft®	Yarn Amount
■ Dk. Royal	#07	#48	20 yds.

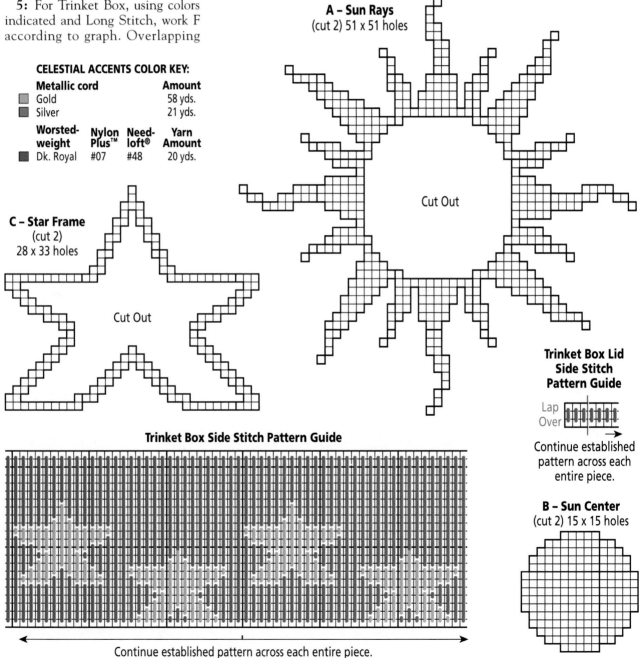

A – Sun Rays
(cut 2) 51 x 51 holes

Cut Out

C – Star Frame
(cut 2)
28 x 33 holes

Cut Out

Trinket Box Lid Side Stitch Pattern Guide

Lap Over

Continue established pattern across each entire piece.

B – Sun Center
(cut 2) 15 x 15 holes

Trinket Box Side Stitch Pattern Guide

Continue established pattern across each entire piece.

I – Trinket Box Bottom
(cut 1)
45 x 45 holes

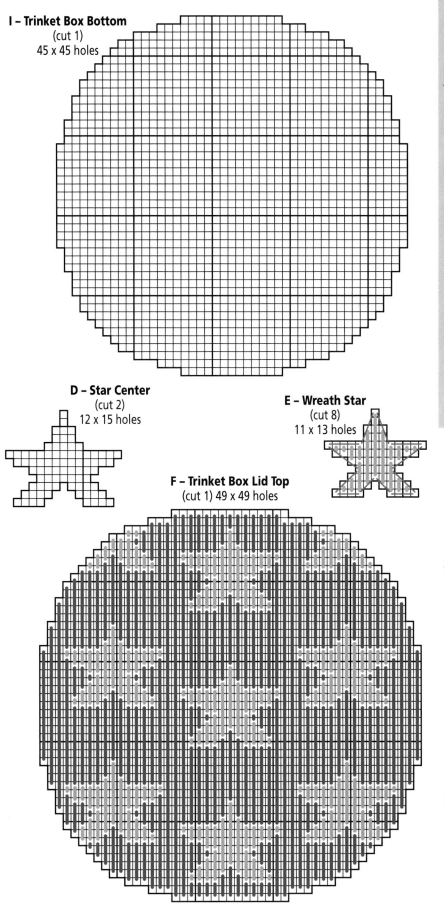

D – Star Center
(cut 2)
12 x 15 holes

E – Wreath Star
(cut 8)
11 x 13 holes

F – Trinket Box Lid Top
(cut 1) 49 x 49 holes

Toy Soldier Quartet
Continued from page 122

Knot, Straight Stitch and Backstitch, embroider facial and uniform detail as indicated on graph. With gold thread, sew beads and bells (see photo) to jacket fronts as indicated.

3: To finish each body, overlapping ends one hole, using matching colors and Continental Stitch, work through both thicknesses as one piece to join.

4: Using colors and stitches indicated, work B-D pieces according to graphs. With metallics for top edge of shoulders and with matching colors, Overcast unfinished edges of C and D pieces. Using metallics, Straight Stitch and Backstitch, embroider sleeve detail as indicated.

5: With matching colors, Whipstitch A and B pieces together. Glue arms and feathers to body as shown.❃

Felt Cutting Illustration
Sheet #1

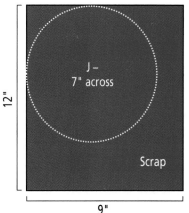

12"

J –
7" across

Scrap

9"

Sheet #2

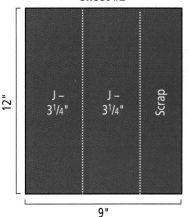

12"

J –
3¼"

J –
3¼"

Scrap

9"

127

A – Initials
(cut letter of choice from 10-count)

B – Bookmark
(cut 1 from colored 7-count)
10 x 48 holes

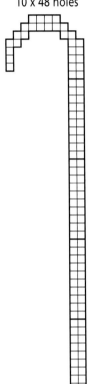

**Monogram Bookmark
Assembly Diagram**
(back view)

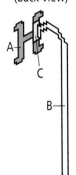

**MONOGRAM BOOKMARKS
COLOR KEY:**

**Medium metallic braid
or floss**	**Amount**
■ Leaf or stripe color	1-2 yds.
■ Flower color	1-1½ yds.

**#3 pearl cotton or
heavy metallic braid**	**Amount**
☐ Background color	3-4 yds.
☐ Overcast color	2-3 yds.

STITCH KEY:
— Backstitch/Straight Stitch
• French Knot/Bead Attachment

Night Jewels Ornaments
Continued from page 125

in next st, (dc, tr, dc) in next st, 2 hdc in next st; repeat from * around, join with sl st in first sl st (20 hdc, 10 dc, 10 sl sts, 5 tr). For **first Side**, fasten off; for **second Side, do not** fasten off.

Rnd 6: Hold Sides wrong sides together, matching sts; working through both thicknesses in **back lps,** sl st in each st around, stuffing with black yarn before closing, fasten off.

Glue blue ribbon rose to center of Star.

Glue ends of blue ribbon to back of Star for hanging loop.

HEART
SIDE (make 2)
Row 1: With cord, ch 2, 3 sc in 2nd ch from hook, turn (3 sc).

Row 2: Ch 1, sc in first st, 2 sc in next st, sc in last st, turn (4).

Rows 3-6: Ch 1, 2 sc in first st, sc in each st across with 2 sc in last st, turn, ending with 12 sts in last row.

Rows 7-8: Ch 1, sc in each st across, turn.

Row 9: Ch 1, (sc, hdc) in first st, *dc in next st, 2 dc in next st, dc in next st*, hdc in next st, sl st in each of next 2 sts, hdc in next st; repeat between **, (hdc, sc) in last st, turn.

Rnd 10: Working around outer edge in sts and in ends of rows, ch 1, sc in each st and in each row around with 3 sc in tip, join with sl st in first sc. For **first Side,** fasten off; for **second Side, do not** fasten off.

Rnd 6: Hold both Sides wrong sides together, matching sts; working through both thicknesses in **back lps,** sl st in each st around, stuffing with black yarn before closing, fasten off.

Glue pink ribbon rose to top of Heart.

Glue ends of pink ribbon to back of Heart for hanging loop.

WREATH
BACK
NOTE: Do not join rnds unless otherwise stated. Mark first st of each rnd.

Rnd 1: With cord, ch 24, sl st in first ch to form ring, ch 1, sc in each ch around (24 sc).

Rnd 2: (Sc in each of next 3 sts, 2 sc in next st) around (30).

Rnd 3: (Sc in next 4 sts, 2 sc in next st) around, join with sl st in first sc, fasten off (36).

FRONT
NOTE: Do not join rnds unless otherwise stated. Mark first st of each rnd.

Rnd 1: With cord, ch 24, sl st in first ch to form ring, ch 1, sc in each ch around (24 sc).

Rnd 2: (Sc in each of next 3 sts, 2 sc in next st) around, join (30).

Rnd 3: (Sc in next 4 sts, 2 sc in next st) around, join with sl st in first sc (36).

Rnd 4: Working this rnd in **front lps,** ch 2, (sl st in next st, ch 2) around, join with sl st in joining sl st of last rnd, fasten off.

Holding Front and Back wrong sides together, matching sts, sew rnd 1 together.

Rnd 5: Working through both thicknesses in **back lps** of rnd 3 on each piece, join with sl st in any st, sl st in each st around, stuffing with black yarn before closing, fasten off.

Glue yellow ribbon rose to top of Wreath.

Glue ends of yellow ribbon to back of Wreath for hanging loop.❀

Quick as a Wink Gifts

Saying "I love you" has never been this easy, or this much fun! When you need just the right present for a really special person, but time is of the essence, these great ideas will save the day. Everything from toys to adult gift items make up this adorable assortment of ten unique products in three different techniques — cross stitch, crochet, and plastic canvas.

Skating Kitties

Designed by Janelle Giese of Janelle Marie Designs

TECHNIQUE:
• Cross Stitch

MATERIALS:
• ½ yd. white 14-count 55" afghan fabric

STITCHING INSTRUCTIONS

NOTE: Trim afghan fabric to 11½" x 55", having a 5⅞" x 6" design area evenly spaced at each short fringed edge. Graph on page 148.

1: Center and stitch design 38 threads from fringe on one short edge of afghan fabric, stitching over two threads and using six strands floss or three strands #317 held together with three strands #3799 for Cross Stitch, and two strands floss for Backstitch of eyes. Use four strands metallic blending filament for Backstitch of skates and ice trail. Use four stands floss for remaining Backstitch. Reverse design on opposite end of scarf if desired.✿

Rosebuds & Ribbons

Designed by Michele Wilcox

CUTTING INSTRUCTIONS

NOTE: Diagram and graphs continued on page 148.

A: For top, cut one according to graph.

B: For sides, cut four (two for sides #1 and two for sides #2) 30 x 36 holes.

C: For bow loops, cut one according to graph.

D: For bow tails, cut one according to graph.

E: For bow knot, cut one 3 x 11 holes (no graph).

STITCHING INSTRUCTIONS

1: Using colors and stitches indicated, work A-D pieces according to graphs.

Using pink and Slanted Gobelin over narrow width, work E.

2: For Cover, with white, Overcast unfinished cutout edges of A. Whipstitch A and B pieces together according to Cover Assembly Diagram.

3: With pink, Overcast unfinished edges of D and unfinished long edges of E. Holding ends of C wrong sides together, Whipstitch together as indicated on graph, forming loops; Overcast unfinished edges.

4: Folding short ends of E wrong sides together over center of loops and tails (see photo), Whipstitch together, forming bow. Glue bow to Cover as shown.❋

TECHNIQUE:
• Plastic Canvas

SIZE:
• Snugly covers a boutique-style tissue box

MATERIALS:
• 1¼ sheets of 7-count plastic canvas
• Craft glue or glue gun
• Worsted-weight or plastic canvas yarn (for amounts see Color Key)

C – Bow Loops (cut 1) 5 x 32 holes

Whipstitch

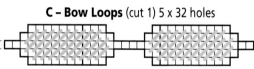

ROSEBUDS & RIBBONS COLOR KEY:

	Worsted-weight	Nylon Plus™	Need-loft®	Yarn Amount
	White	#01	#41	50 yds.
	Sea Green	#37	#53	32 yds.
	Pink	#11	#07	18 yds.
	Rose	#12	#06	10 yds.
	Straw	#41	#19	3 yds.

B – Side #1 (cut 2) 30 x 36 holes

Circus Sock Pals

Designed by Debbie Tabor

TECHNIQUE:
- Plastic Canvas

SIZE:
- Each doll is about 16" long

MATERIALS FOR ONE OF EACH:
- Four sheets of 7-count plastic canvas
- One yellow and one gray child-size stocking
- Cotton balls, polyester fiberfill, candy or other stocking stuffer
- Sewing needle and matching color thread
- Craft glue or glue gun
- Metallic cord (for amount see Clown Color Key on page 137)
- Six-strand embroidery floss (for amounts see individual Color Keys on pages 136 & 137)
- Worsted-weight or plastic canvas yarn (for amounts see individual Color Keys)

LION
CUTTING INSTRUCTIONS
NOTE: Graphs on page 136.

A: For head front and back, cut one each according to graphs.

B: For muzzle, cut one according to graph.

C: For arm tops and bottoms, cut two each according to graphs.

D: For leg tops and bottoms, cut two each according to graphs.

STITCHING INSTRUCTIONS
1: Using colors indicated, Continental Stitch and Cross Stitch, work front A and B-D pieces according to graphs; fill in uncoded areas of A-D pieces using yellow and Continental Stitch. Using yarn and six strands floss in colors indicated, Backstitch, Straight Stitch and French Knot, embroider detail as indicated on graphs.

2: Using gold and Rya Knot (see Stitch Illustration), work A pieces according to graphs.

3: With black, Overcast unfinished side edges of B as indicated. With white, Whipstitch muzzle to front A as indicated; Overcast remaining unfinished edges of muzzle. With black for front and with gold, Overcast remaining cutout edges of A pieces.

4: For head, holding A pieces wrong sides together, with matching colors, Whipstitch together. For mane, clip through Rya Knot loops; fray ends to fluff.

5: To shape arms, holding wrist edges of each top C right side together, with white, Whipstitch cutout edges together tightly according to graph; holding edges of each bottom C wrong sides together, Whipstitch cutout edges together loosely according to graph.

6: For each arm, holding one of each C wrong sides together, with matching colors, Whipstitch together.

7: To shape ankles on legs, Whipstitch cutout edges of D pieces together as in Step 5. To shape knees, holding edges of each top D wrong sides together, with yellow, Whipstitch cutout edges together loosely according to graph; holding edges of each bottom D right sides together, Whipstitch cutout edges together tightly according to graph.

8: For each leg, Whipstitch one of each D together as for arms in Step 6.

9: Stuff stocking; fold ankle edge down, and sew folded edge to cutout edges of head back. Sew arms and legs to stocking as shown in photo.

CLOWN
CUTTING INSTRUCTIONS:
NOTE: Graphs and diagram on page 137.

A: For head front and back, cut one each according to graphs.

B: For cheeks, cut one according to graph.

C: For arm #1 and #2 tops and bottoms, cut two each according to graphs.

D: For leg tops and bottoms, cut two each according to graphs.

E: For cuffs, cut four according to graph.

STITCHING INSTRUCTIONS
1: Using colors indicated and Continental Stitch, work A-C (one of each C#1 and C#2 on opposite side of canvas), D and two E pieces according to graphs; substituting purple for lime, work remaining E pieces. Using orange and Rya Knot (see Stitch Illustration), work A pieces according to graphs.

2: Using six strands floss in colors indicated, Backstitch and French Knot, embroider detail as indicated on front A, B and top D graphs. Using metallic cord and Straight Stitch and starting and stopping at indicated holes (see Shoe Lacing Diagram), embroider as indicated; tie laces into bows.

3: With white, Whipstitch cheeks to front A as indicated; with red, Overcast unfinished edges of muzzle and cutout edges of front A. With matching colors, Overcast cutout edges of back A.

4: For head, holding A pieces wrong sides together, with matching colors, Whipstitch together.

5: To shape wrists on arms, holding wrist edges of each top C right sides together, with indicated color, Whipstitch cutout edges together tightly according to graph; holding wrist edges of each bottom C wrong sides together, Whipstitch cutout edges together loosely. To shape elbows, Whipstitch cutout edges together as for wrists.

6: For each arm, holding one top and one bottom C wrong sides together, with silver for sleeves and with white, Whipstitch together.

7: To shape legs, with silver, follow Step 7 of Lion.

8: For each leg, holding one top and one
Continued on page 136

bottom D wrong sides together, with black for shoes and with silver, Whipstitch together.

9: For each cuff, holding matching-color E pieces wrong sides together, with matching color, Whipstitch side edges together as indicated; with matching color for wrist edges and with contrasting color for cuff edges, Overcast unfinished edges. Slip cuffs on arm as shown in photo.

NOTE: Cut remaining red, purple and lime into 4-yd. lengths.

10: For each pom-pom, wrap one 4-

LION SOCK PAL COLOR KEY:

Embroidery floss			Amount
■ Black			3 yds.

Worsted-weight	Nylon Plus™	Need-loft®	Yarn Amount
▨ Yellow	#26	#57	38 yds.
▢ White	#01	#41	27 yds.
▨ Gold	#27	#17	26 yds.
▨ Black	#02	#00	6 yds.
▨ Green	#58	#28	1/4 yd.

STITCH KEY:
- — Backstitch/Straight Stitch
- ● French Knot
- ◠ Rya Knot
- ▢ Muzzle Attachment

C – Lion Arm Bottom
(cut 2) 18 x 39 holes
Cut out gray area carefully.

A – Lion Head Front
(cut 1)
32 x 32 holes

Cut Out

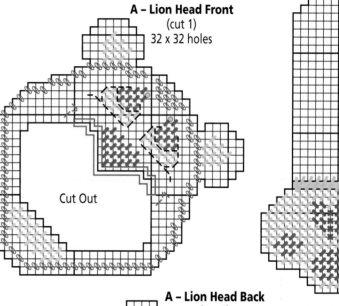

A – Lion Head Back
(cut 1)
32 x 32 holes

Cut Out

D – Lion Leg Top
(cut 2) 20 x 52 holes
Cut out gray areas carefully.

C – Lion Arm Top
(cut 2) 18 x 39 holes
Cut out gray area carefully.

D – Lion Leg Bottom
(cut 2) 20 x 52 holes
Cut out gray areas carefully.

Overcast with black.

B – Lion Muzzle
(cut 1)
17 x 17 holes

Overcast with black.

Rya Knot Stitch Illustration

1 2 5 6
3 4 7

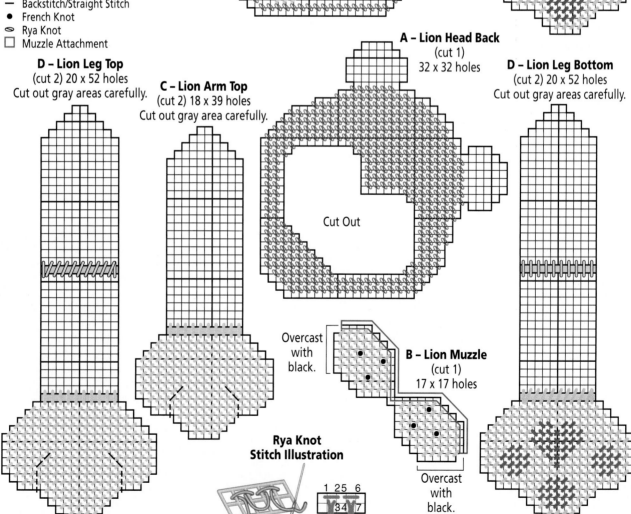

yd. strand around two fingers; tie separate strand tightly around center of all loops. Cut loops and pull ends into a round shape around knot; trim ends to form a 1¼"-1½" pom-pom.

11: Stuff stocking; fold ankle edge down, and sew folded edge to cutout edges of head back. Sew arms and legs to stocking as shown. Glue red pom-pom to face for nose and remaining pom-poms to cuff for collar (see photo).❈

Shoe Lacing Diagram
(Shoe top Continental Stitches not shown for clarity.)

Step 1:
Start here.

Shoe Top

Step 2:
Continue lacing stitches to indicated hole according to graph.

C – Clown Arm #1 Top & Bottom
(cut 1 each) 19 x 41 holes
Cut out gray areas carefully.

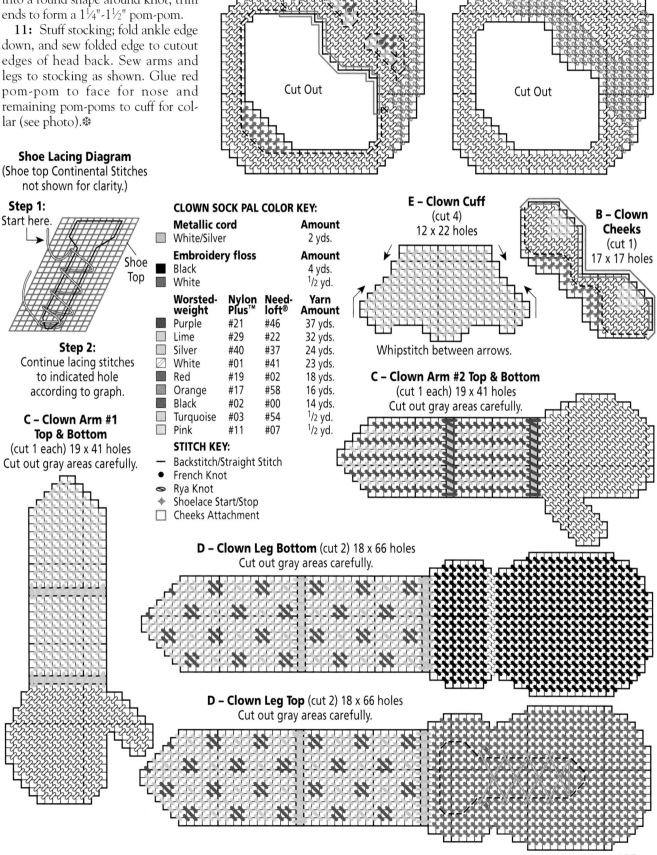

A – Clown Head Front (cut 1) 26 x 26 holes

Cut Out

A – Clown Head Back (cut 1) 26 x 26 holes

Cut Out

CLOWN SOCK PAL COLOR KEY:

Metallic cord			Amount
White/Silver			2 yds.

Embroidery floss			Amount
Black			4 yds.
White			½ yd.

Worsted-weight	Nylon Plus™	Need-loft®	Yarn Amount
Purple	#21	#46	37 yds.
Lime	#29	#22	32 yds.
Silver	#40	#37	24 yds.
White	#01	#41	23 yds.
Red	#19	#02	18 yds.
Orange	#17	#58	16 yds.
Black	#02	#00	14 yds.
Turquoise	#03	#54	½ yd.
Pink	#11	#07	½ yd.

STITCH KEY:
— Backstitch/Straight Stitch
● French Knot
〜 Rya Knot
✦ Shoelace Start/Stop
▢ Cheeks Attachment

E – Clown Cuff
(cut 4)
12 x 22 holes

Whipstitch between arrows.

B – Clown Cheeks
(cut 1)
17 x 17 holes

C – Clown Arm #2 Top & Bottom
(cut 1 each) 19 x 41 holes
Cut out gray areas carefully.

D – Clown Leg Bottom (cut 2) 18 x 66 holes
Cut out gray areas carefully.

D – Clown Leg Top (cut 2) 18 x 66 holes
Cut out gray areas carefully.

Winter Warmers

Designed by Shari L. Jacobson

TECHNIQUE:
• Crochet

SIZE:
• Girl's Neck Wrap is 22" long not including tassel
• Girl's Ear Warmer is 24½" long
• Boy's Neck Wrap is 19" long not including tassel
• Boy's Ear Warmer is 20" long

MATERIALS FOR ALL FOUR:
• Fuzzy worsted-weight yarn — 4½ oz. red
• 3½ oz. blue and 2 oz white
• 6 white 20-mm buttons
• Tapestry needle
• I crochet hook or size needed to obtain gauge

GAUGE:
• 3 dc sts = 1"
• 2 dc rows = 1½"
• 3 sc = 1"
• 3 sc back lp rows = 1"

GIRL'S NECK WRAP

NOTES: For best results, practice spike cluster before beginning Wrap.

For **spike cluster (spike cl),** working loosely, insert hook in st two sts to right and one row down, yo, draw lp through, insert hook in st one st to right and two rows down, yo, draw lp through, insert hook in st three rows down, yo, draw lp through, insert hook in st one st to left and 2 rows down, yo, draw lp through, insert hook in st two sts to left and one row down, yo, draw lp through, insert hook in next st on this row, yo, draw lp through, yo, draw through all 7 lps on hook.

Row 1: With red, ch 48, sc in 2nd ch from hook, sc in each ch across, turn (47 sc).

Rows 2-4: Working these rows in **back lps** only, ch 1, sc in each st across, turn.

Rows 5-7: Ch 1, sc in each st across, turn. At end of last row, fasten off.

Row 8: Join white with sc in first st, sc in next 6 sts, (spike cl, sc in next 7 sts) across, turn.

Rows 9-11: Ch 1, sc in each st across, turn. At end of last row, fasten off.

Row 12: Join red with sc in first st, sc in each of next 2 sts, (spike cl, sc in next 7 sts) across to last 4 sts, spike cl, sc in each of last 3 sts, turn.

Rows 13-15: Ch 1, sc in each st across, turn.

Rows 16-18: Working these rows in **back lps** only, ch 1, sc in each st across, turn. At end of last row, **do not** turn.

Row 19: For **first end,** ch 1, evenly space 12 sc across ends of rows, turn.

NOTE: Work remaining rows in **back lps** only.

Rows 20-26: Ch 1, sc in each st across, turn.

Row 27: Ch 1, sc first 2 sts tog, sc in each st across to last 2 sts, sc last 2 sts tog, turn (10).

Row 28: For **tassel loop,** ch 5; sc first 2 sts tog, sc in each st across to last 2 sts, sc last 2 sts tog, turn (8).

Rows 29-30: Repeat row 27. At end of last row, fasten off.

Row 31: For **second end,** working on opposite end, join red with sc in end of first row, evenly space 11 more sc across ends of rows, turn (12 sc).

Rows 32-38: Ch 1, sc in each st across, turn.

Row 39: Ch 1, sc first 2 sts tog, sc in each of next 3 sts; for **buttonhole,** ch 2, skip next 2 sts; sc in each of next 3 sts, sc last 2 sts tog, turn.

Row 40: Ch 1, sc first 2 sts tog, sc in each st and in each ch across to last 2 sts, sc last 2 sts tog, turn (8).

Rows 41-42: Repeat row 27. At end of last row, fasten off.

With right side facing you, sew button centered to row 26 on first end.

TASSEL

Cut 12 strands red each 20" long. Pull one end of all strands held together through tassel loop, pull to even. Tie separate strand red around all ends 1" from fold; secure ends.

GIRL'S EAR WARMER

Rows 1-18: Work same rows of Girl's Neck Wrap. At end of last row, **turn.**

Row 19: Working this row in **back lps** only, ch 1, sc in first 13 sts, hdc in next 5 sts, dc in next st, dc next 2 sts tog, dc in each of next 2 sts, 3 dc in next st, dc in each of next 2 sts, dc next 2 sts tog, dc in next st, hdc in next 5 sts, sc in last 13 sts, turn.

Row 20: Working this row in **back lps** only, ch 1, sc in first 13 sts, hdc in next 5 sts, dc in next 5 sts, (dc, ch 2, dc) in next st, dc in next 5 sts, hdc in next 5 sts, sc in last 13 sts, **do not** turn.

Row 21: For **first end,** ch 1, evenly space 12 sc across ends of rows, turn.

NOTE: Work remaining rows in **back lps** only.

Rows 22-24: Ch 1, sc in each st across, turn.

Rows 25-28: Ch 1, sc first 2 sts tog, sc in each st across to last 2 sts, sc last 2 sts tog, turn, ending with 4 sts in last row.

Row 29: Ch 1, (sc next 2 sts tog) 2 times, fasten off.

Row 30: For **second end,** working on opposite end, join with sc in first row, evenly space 11 more sc across ends of rows, turn (12 sc).

Rows 31-38: Repeat rows 22-29, **do not** fasten off.

Row 39: For **buttonhole strap,** ch 16, sc in 2nd ch from hook, sc in each ch across, sl st in first st on row 38, turn.

Row 40: (Ch 2, skip next 2 sts, sc in next st) 5 times, turn.

Row 41: Ch 1, sc in each st and 2 sc in each ch-2 sp across, sl st in last st on row 38, fasten off.

Sew two buttons centered on rows 4 and 7 of first end.

TASSEL

Cut 12 strands red each 20" long. Pull one end of all strands held together through ch-2 sp on row 20, pull to even. Tie separate strand red around all ends 1" from fold; secure ends.

BOY'S NECK WRAP

Row 1: With blue, ch 50, sc in 2nd ch from hook, sc in each ch across, turn (49 sc).

Row 2: Working this row in **back lps** only, ch 1, sc in each of first 2 sts, (ch 1, skip next st, sc in each of next 3 sts) across to last 3 sts, ch 1, skip next st, sc in each of last 2 sts, turn.

Row 3: Ch 3, dc in next st, ch 1, skip next ch sp, (dc in each of next 3 sts, ch 1, skip next ch sp) across to last 2 sts, dc in each of last 2 sts, turn, fasten off.

Row 4: Join white with sc in first st, sc in next st, (tr in next ch-1 sp on row before last, skip next ch sp on last row, sc in next st, ch 1, skip next st, sc in next st) 11 times, tr in next ch-1 sp on row before last, skip next ch sp on last row, sc in each of last 2 sts, turn.

Row 5: Ch 3, dc in each of next 3 sts, (ch 1, skip next st, dc in each of next 3 sts) across to last st, dc in last st, turn, fasten off.

Row 6: Join red with sc in first st,
Continued on page 149

Keepsake Gift Tags

Designed by Celia Lange Designs

TECHNIQUE:
• Plastic Canvas

SIZE:
• Each is about 1½" x 2⅞"

MATERIALS:
• Two sheets of 14-count plastic canvas
• ¹⁄₁₆" metallic ribbon or heavy metallic braid (for amount see Color Key)
• Six-strand embroidery floss (for amounts see Color Key)

CUTTING INSTRUCTIONS

A: For tag #1 front and back, cut one each according to graph.

B: For tag #2 front and back, cut one each according to graph.

C: For tag #3 front and back, cut one each according to graph.

D: For tag #4 front and back, cut one each according to graph.

E: For tag #5 front and back, cut one each according to graph.

F: For tag #6 front and back, cut one each according to graph.

STITCHING INSTRUCTIONS

NOTE: Separate floss into 3-ply strands.

1: Using white for Tags #1 & #2, red for Tags #3 & #4, green for Tags #5 & #6 and Cross Stitch, work A-F (work backs above blue line only as indicated on graphs) pieces.

2: With matching colors, Overcast unfinished cutout edges of A-F pieces; Overcast unfinished top edges of front A-F pieces (see photo).

3: Using colors indicated, Back-stitch, Straight Stitch, French Knot and Lazy Daisy Stitch, embroider detail (see Woven Backstitch Diagram) as indicated on graphs.

4: For each tag, holding front and back pieces wrong sides together at matching bottom edges, Whipstitch together as indicated; Overcast unfinished edges.❄

A – Tag #1 Front   A – Tag #1 Back
(cut 1) 21 x 25 holes   (cut 1) 21 x 34 holes

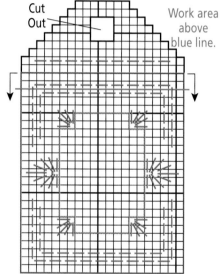

Whipstitch between arrows.

C – Tag #3 Front   C – Tag #3 Back
(cut 1) 25 x 30 holes   (cut 1) 25 x 38 holes

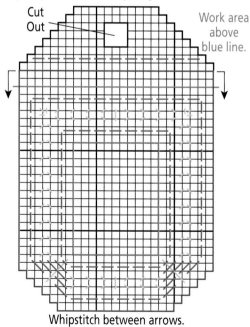

Whipstitch between arrows.

B – Tag #2 Front   B – Tag #2 Back
(cut 1) 19 x 29 holes   (cut 1) 19 x 36 holes

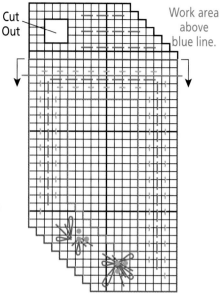

Whipstitch between arrows.

F – Tag #6 Front   F – Tag #6 Back
(cut 1) 20 x 31 holes   (cut 1) 20 x 34 holes

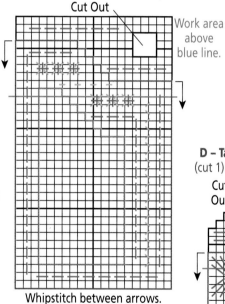

Whipstitch between arrows.

GIFT TAGS COLOR KEY:

1/16" metallic ribbon or braid	Amount
▨ Gold	3 yds.
Embroidery floss	**Amount**
■ Red	18 yds.
■ Green	16 yds.
▨ White	14 yds.

STITCH KEY:
- ☐ Cut Out For Front Only
- — Backstitch/Straight Stitch
- ● French Knot
- ◠ Lazy Daisy Stitch

E – Tag #5 Front   E – Tag #5 Back
(cut 1) 19 x 27 holes   (cut 1) 19 x 35 holes

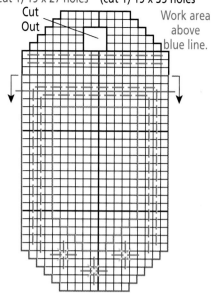

Whipstitch between arrows.

Woven Backstitch Diagram

Step 1:
Work Backstitches as indicated on graphs.

Step 2:
Weave a contrasting color of choice through stitches; secure ends at back.

D – Tag #4 Front   D – Tag #4 Back
(cut 1) 21 x 29 holes   (cut 1) 21 x 38 holes

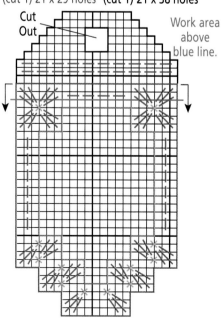

Whipstitch between arrows.

141

TECHNIQUE:
- Plastic Canvas

SIZE:
- 6" x 15"

MATERIALS:
- One sheet of 7-count plastic canvas
- ⅓ yd. pink ⅜" satin ribbon
- Craft glue or glue gun
- #3 pearl cotton or six-strand embroidery floss (for amount see Color Key)
- Worsted-weight or plastic canvas yarn (for amounts see Color Key)

Cat & Mouse

Designed by Michele Wilcox

CUTTING INSTRUCTIONS

A: For cat body, cut one according to graph.

B: For cat head, cut one according to graph.

C: For cat tail, cut one according to graph on page 149.

D: For mouse body, cut one according to graph on page 149.

E: For mouse ears #1 & #2, cut one each according to graphs.

STITCHING INSTRUCTIONS

NOTE: Use Continental Stitch throughout.

A - Cat Body (cut 1) 33 x 70 holes

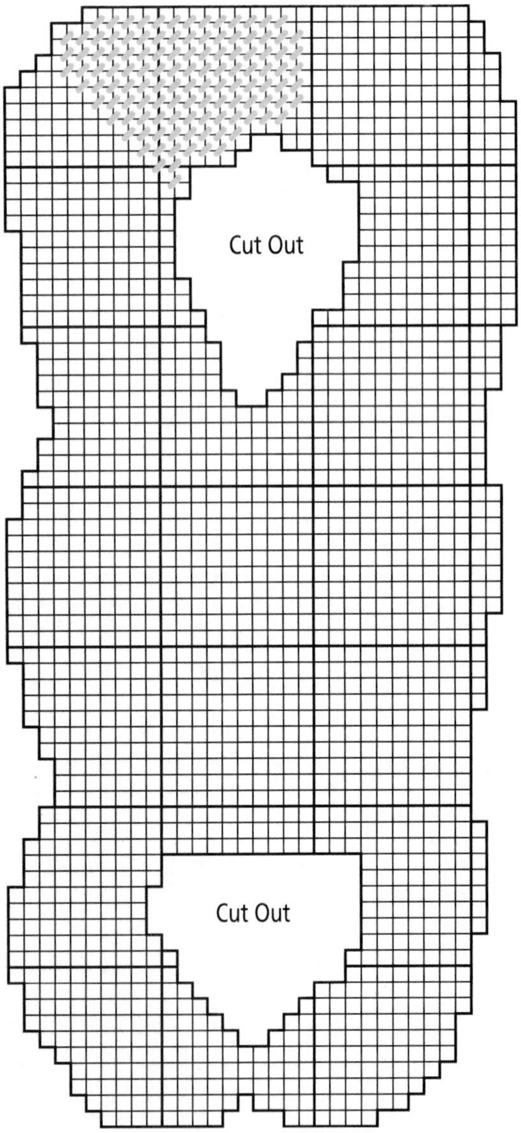

1: Using colors indicated, work A-C pieces according to graphs; fill in uncoded areas using black. With black for ears and with matching colors, Overcast unfinished edges of A-C pieces. Using black, Straight Stitch and French Knot, embroider facial detail as indicated on B graph.

2: Using colors indicated, work D and E pieces according to graphs; with silver, Overcast unfinished edges, leaving about 10" hanging at top of mouse body for tail. Using pearl cotton or six strands floss and French Knot, embroider eyes as indicated on D graph.

3: Tie ribbon into a bow around cat's tail as shown in photo; trim ends. Glue head and tail to cat's body and ears to mouse's body as shown. Tie mouse's tail around cat's paws as shown.❄

B - Cat Head (cut 1) 22 x 23 holes

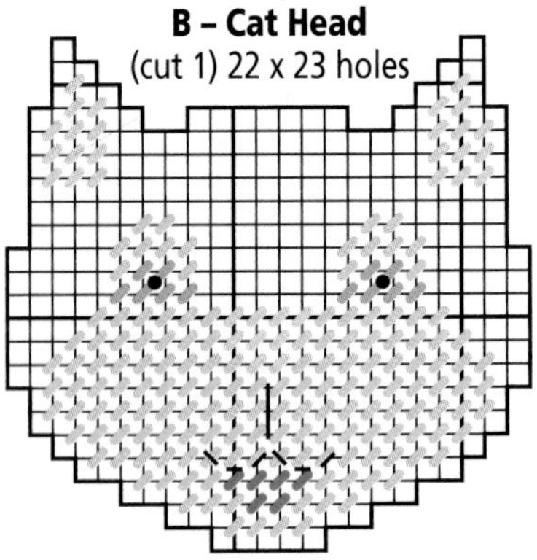

E - Mouse Ear #1 (cut 1) 7 x 7 holes

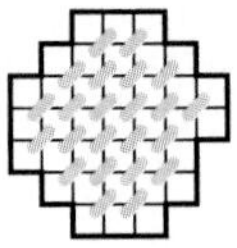

E - Mouse Ear #2 (cut 1) 7 x 7 holes

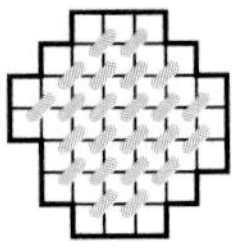

CAT & MOUSE COLOR KEY:

#3 pearl cotton or floss			Amount
Black			1/4 yd.
Worsted-weight	**Nylon Plus™**	**Need-loft®**	**Yarn Amount**
Black	#02	#00	30 yds.
White	#01	#41	6 yds.
Silver	#40	#37	4 yds.
Pink	#11	#07	2 yds.
Lime	#29	#22	1/2 yd.
Red	#19	#02	1/4 yd.

STITCH KEY:
- — Backstitch/Straight Stitch
- ● French Knot

Globe Game

Designed by Carol Nartowicz

CUTTING INSTRUCTIONS

A: For handle sides, cut two from 7-count according to graph.

B: For game piece, cut two from 10-count according to graph.

STITCHING INSTRUCTIONS

1: Using yarn in colors indicated and Continental Stitch, work A pieces according to graph. Holding A pieces wrong sides together, with white, Whipstitch together.

2: Using blue and yellow pearl cotton or six strands floss and stitches indicated, work one B piece in each color according to graph. Holding B pieces wrong sides together, with red, Whipstitch together.

NOTE: Carefully break off loop on craft globe; file down rough edges.

3: Open craft globe. Place blue beads and game piece inside one globe half; glue globe together, inserting yellow beads in opposite half of globe before closing (see photo). Glue globe inside center cutout of handle as shown.❈

B – Game Piece
(cut 2 from 10-count) 29 x 29 holes

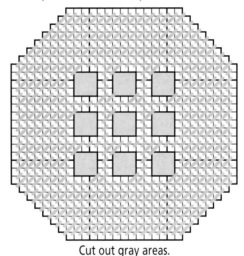

Cut out gray areas.

A – Handle Side
(cut 2 from 7-count) 51 x 51 holes

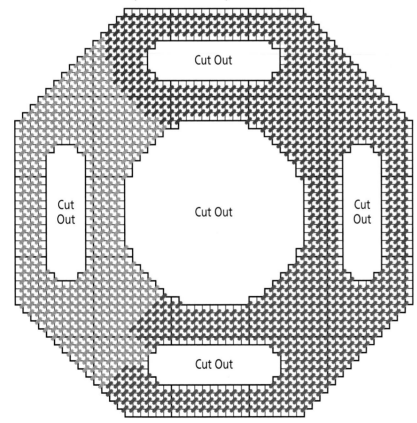

TECHNIQUE:
• Plastic Canvas

SIZE:
• 7¾" across

MATERIALS:
• Two sheets of 7-count plastic canvas
• ½ sheet of 10-count plastic canvas
• One clear/clear craft globe
• Five each yellow and blue 6-mm round beads
• Craft glue or glue gun
• #3 pearl cotton or six-strand embroidery floss (for amounts see Color Key)
• Worsted-weight or plastic canvas yarn (for amounts see Color Key)

PRIMARIES GLOBE GAME COLOR KEY:

#3 pearl cotton or floss			Amount
☐ Blue			6 yds.
▨ Yellow			6 yds.
☐ Red			4 yds.

Worsted-weight	Nylon Plus™	Need-loft®	Yarn Amount
■ Red	#19	#02	16 yds.
■ Royal	#09	#32	16 yds.
▨ Yellow	#26	#57	15 yds.
☐ White	#01	#41	8 yds.

Sweetheart Treasure Box

Designed by Carol Nartowicz

TECHNIQUE:
• Plastic Canvas

SIZE:
• 5¼" x 7¼" x 3¼" tall

MATERIALS:
• Two sheets each of black and pink 7-count plastic canvas
• Two pink 9" x 12" sheets of felt (optional)
• 28 pearl 4-mm beads
• One pearl 10-mm sew-on button
• One pink 1½" satin ribbon rose
• Sewing needle and pink thread
• Craft glue or glue gun
• ⅛" satin ribbon (for amount see Color Key)
• Worsted-weight or plastic canvas yarn (for amounts see Color Key)

CUTTING INSTRUCTIONS

A: For lid and lining, cut one from black according to graph and one from pink 33 x 47 holes (no lining graph).

B: For box sides and linings, cut two from black according to graph and two from pink 19 x 47 holes (no lining graph).

C: For box ends and linings, cut two from black according to graph and two from pink 19 x 33 holes (no lining graph).

D: For box bottom and lining, cut two (one from black and one from pink) 33 x 47 holes (no graphs).

E: For optional box felt linings, using lining B-D pieces as patterns, cut one each from felt ⅛" smaller at all edges.

Box Assembly Diagram

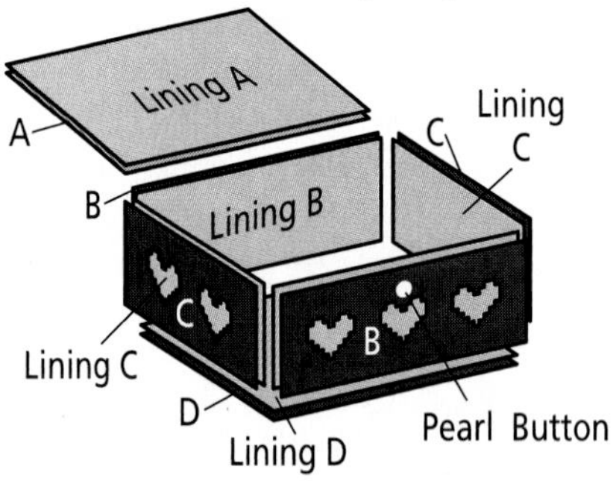
Lining A
A
Lining C
C
Lining B
B
C
B
Lining C
D
Lining D
Pearl Button

STITCHING INSTRUCTIONS

NOTE: Lining A and B-D pieces are unworked.

1: Using lt. pink and Continental Stitch, work A according to graph. With thread, sew on button as indicated on B graph; with black, Whipstitch A-D pieces together as indicated and according to Box Assembly Diagram. Glue E pieces inside box.

NOTE: Cut one 20" length of ribbon.

2: Using 20" ribbon and stitches indicated, working through both thicknesses as one and starting and ending on lid as indicated, work A according to graph. Pull ends of ribbon to even and tie into a bow; trim ends.

3: For closure loop, thread ends of remaining ribbon from front to back through ♦ holes as indicated on lid top (see photo); knot ends together on wrong side to secure. Glue pearl beads and rose to lid as indicated and as shown.❈

A – Lid (cut 1 from black) 33 x 47 holes

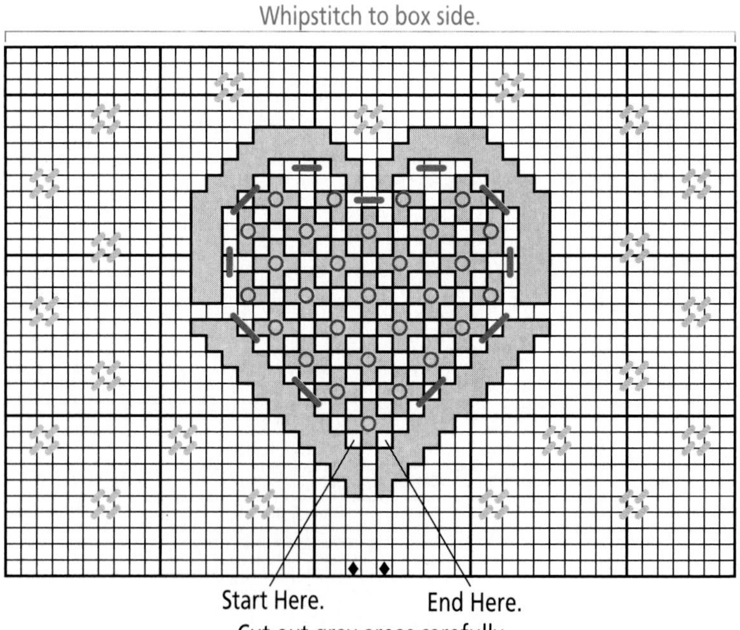
Whipstitch to box side.
Start Here.
End Here.
Cut out gray areas carefully.

SWEETHEART BOX COLOR KEY:

1/8" ribbon			Amount
■ Pink			1 yd.

Worsted-weight	Nylon Plus™	Need-loft®	Yarn Amount
□ Black	#02	#00	10 yds.
□ Lt. Pink	#10	#08	2 yds.

STITCH KEY:
X Button Attachment
♦ Ribbon Attachment
○ Bead Placement

C – Box End
(cut 2 from black) 19 x 33 holes

B – Box Side
(cut 2 from black) 19 x 47 holes

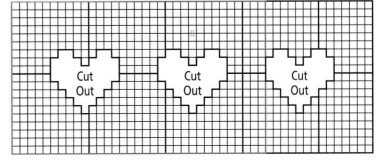

147

Skating Kitties Instructions on page 132

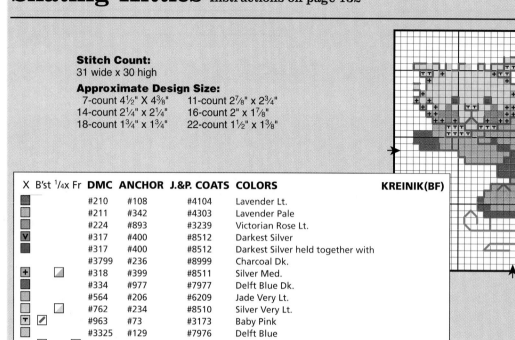

Stitch Count:
31 wide x 30 high

Approximate Design Size:
7-count 4½" X 4⅜"   11-count 2⅞" x 2¾"
14-count 2¼" x 2¼"   16-count 2" x 1⅞"
18-count 1¾" x 1¾"   22-count 1½" x 1⅜"

X	B'st	¼x	Fr	DMC	ANCHOR	J.&P. COATS	COLORS	KREINIK(BF)
■				#210	#108	#4104	Lavender Lt.	
▨				#211	#342	#4303	Lavender Pale	
▨				#224	#893	#3239	Victorian Rose Lt.	
V				#317	#400	#8512	Darkest Silver	
■				#317	#400	#8512	Darkest Silver held together with	
				#3799	#236	#8999	Charcoal Dk.	
+		◨		#318	#399	#8511	Silver Med.	
▨				#334	#977	#7977	Delft Blue Dk.	
▨				#564	#206	#6209	Jade Very Lt.	
▨		◨		#762	#234	#8510	Silver Very Lt.	
T	◨			#963	#73	#3173	Baby Pink	
▨				#3325	#129	#7976	Delft Blue	
	◨		◉	#3799	#236	#8999	Charcoal Dk.	
	◨							#001HL Silver

Rosebuds & Ribbons Instructions on page 133

Cover Assembly Diagram
(Pieces shown in different colors for contrast.)

Step 1:
With matching colors, Whipstitch A and B pieces together.

Step 2:
With white, Overcast unfinished bottom edges.

ROSEBUDS & RIBBONS COLOR KEY:

	Worsted-weight	Nylon Plus™	Need-loft®	Yarn Amount
▨	White	#01	#41	50 yds.
■	Sea Green	#37	#53	32 yds.
▨	Pink	#11	#07	18 yds.
■	Rose	#12	#06	10 yds.
▨	Straw	#41	#19	3 yds.

D – Bow Tails
(cut 1)
5 x 22 holes

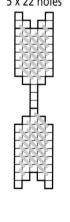

B – Side #2 (cut 2) 30 x 36 holes

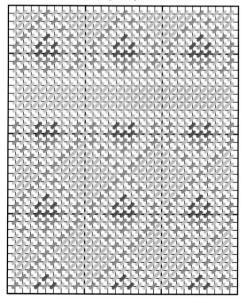

A – Top (cut 1) 30 x 30 holes

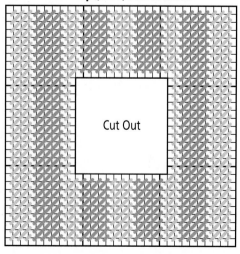

Cut Out

148

(sc in next st, ch 1, skip next st, sc in next st, tr in next ch-1 sp on row before last, skip next ch sp on last row) 11 times, sc in next st, ch 1, skip next st, sc in each of last 2 sts, turn.

Row 7: Ch 3, dc in next st, (ch 1, skip next st, dc in each of next 3 sts) 11 times, ch 1, skip next st, dc in each of last 2 sts, turn, fasten off.

Row 8: With blue, repeat row 4.

Row 9: Ch 3, dc in each st and in each ch across, turn.

Row 10: Working this row in **back lps** only, ch 1, sc in each st across, **do not** turn.

Row 11: For **first end,** evenly space 12 sc across ends of rows, turn (12 sc).

NOTE: Work remaining rows in **back lps** only.

Rows 12-14: Ch 1, sc in each st across, turn.

Row 15: For **tassel loop,** ch 5; sc first 2 sts tog, sc in each st across to last 2 sts, sc last 2 sts tog, turn (10).

Rows 16-18: Ch 1, sc first 2 sts tog, sc in each st across to last 2 sts, sc last 2 sts tog, turn (8, 6, 4). At end of last row, fasten off.

Row 19: For **second end,** working on opposite end, join with sc in end of first row, evenly space 11 more sc across ends of rows, turn (12 sc).

Rows 20-22: Ch 1, sc in each st across, turn.

Row 23: Ch 1, sc first 2 sts tog, sc in each of next 3 sts; for **buttonhole,** ch 2, skip next 2 sts; sc in each of next 3 sts, sc last 2 sts tog

Row 24: Ch 1, sc first 2 sts tog, sc in each st and 2 sc in ch sp across to last 2 sts, sc last 2 sts tog, turn.

Rows 25-26: Repeat row 16. At end of last row, fasten off.

Sew one button centered on row 5 of first end.

TASSEL

Cut 12 strands blue each 20" long. Pull one end of all strands held together through tassel loop, pull to even. Tie separate strand blue around all ends 1" from fold; secure ends.

BOY'S EAR WARMER

Row 1: With blue, ch 42, sc in 2nd ch from hook, sc in next ch, (ch 1, skip next ch, sc in each of next 3 chs) across to last 3 chs, ch 1, skip next ch, sc in each of last 2 chs, turn (31 sc, 10 ch sps).

Row 2: Ch 3, dc in next st, ch 1, skip next ch sp, (dc in each of next 3 sts, ch 1, skip next ch sp) across to last 2 sts, dc in each of last 2 sts, turn, fasten off.

Row 3: Join white with sc in first st, sc in next st, (tr in next ch-1 sp on row before last, skip next ch sp on last row, sc in next st, ch 1, skip next st, sc in next st) 9 times, tr in next ch-1 sp on row before last, skip next ch sp on last row, sc in each of last 2 sts, turn.

Row 4: Ch 3, dc in each of next 3 sts, (ch 1, skip next st, dc in each of next 3 sts) across to last st, dc in last st, turn, fasten off.

Row 5: Join red with sc in first st, (sc in next st, ch 1, skip next st, sc in next st, tr in next ch-1 sp on row before last, skip next ch sp on last row) 9 times, sc in next st, ch 1, skip next st, sc in each of last 2 sts, turn.

Row 6: Ch 3, dc in next st, (ch 1, skip next st, dc in each of next 3 sts) 9 times, ch 1, skip next st, dc in each of last 2 sts, turn, fasten off.

Row 7: With blue, repeat row 3.

Row 8: Ch 3, dc in each st and in each ch across, **do not** turn.

Row 9: For **first end,** evenly space 8 sc across ends of rows, turn (8 sc).

NOTE: Work remaining rows in **back lps** only.

Rows 10-12: Ch 1, sc in each st across, turn.

Rows 13-14: Ch 1, sc first 2 sts tog, sc in each st across to last 2 sts, sc last 2 sts tog, turn.

Row 15: Ch 1, (sc next 2 sts tog) 2 times, fasten off.

Row 16: For **second end,** working on opposite end, join with sc in end of first row, evenly space 7 more sc across ends of rows, turn (8 sc).

Rows 17-22: Repeat rows 10-15, **do not** fasten off.

Row 23: For **buttonhole strap,** ch 10, sc in 2nd ch from hook, sc in next ch, (ch 1, skip next ch, sc in each of next 3 chs) across to last 3 chs, ch 1, skip next ch, sc in each of last 2 chs, turn (31 sc, 10 ch sps).

each ch across, sl st in first st on row 22, turn.

Row 24: (Ch 2, skip next 2 sts, sc in next st) across, turn.

Row 25: Ch 1, sc in each st and in each ch across, sl st in last st on row 22, fasten off.

With right side facing you, sew two buttons centered on rows 10 and 14 of first end.❄

Cat & Mouse
Instructions on page 142

CAT & MOUSE COLOR KEY:

#3 pearl cotton or floss			Amount
■ Black			1/4 yd.

Worsted-weight	Nylon Plus™	Need-loft®	Yarn Amount
■ Black	#02	#00	30 yds.
▢ White	#01	#41	6 yds.
▨ Silver	#40	#37	4 yds.
▨ Pink	#11	#07	2 yds.
▨ Lime	#29	#22	1/2 yd.
▨ Red	#19	#02	1/4 yd.

STITCH KEY:
- — Backstitch/Straight Stitch
- ● French Knot

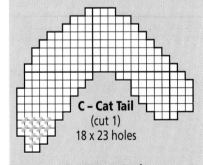

C – Cat Tail
(cut 1)
18 x 23 holes

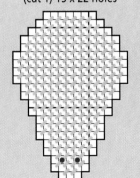

D – Mouse Body
(cut 1) 15 x 22 holes

Basic Instructions to Get You Started

Most needlecrafters love getting their projects organized before they even step out the door in search of supplies. A few moments of careful planning can make the creation of your project even more fun.

First of all, prepare your work area. You will need a flat surface for cutting and assembly, and you will need a place to store your materials. Good lighting is essential, and a comfortable chair will make your stitching time even more enjoyable.

Do you plan to make one project, or will you be making several of the same item? A materials list appears at the beginning of each pattern. If you plan to make several of the same item, multiply your materials accordingly.

Supplies

Yarn, canvas, needles, cutters and most other supplies needed to complete the projects in this book are available through craft and needlework stores and mail order catalogs. Other supplies are available at fabric, hardware and discount stores. For mail order information, see page 160.

Canvas

Most projects can be made using standard-size sheets of canvas. Standard-size sheets of 7-count (7 holes per inch) are 70 x 90 holes and are about 10½" x 13½". For larger projects, 7-count canvas also comes in 12" x 18" (80 x 120 holes) and 13½" x 22½" (90 x 150 holes) sheets. Other shapes are available in 7-count, including circles, diamonds, ovals and purse forms.

10-count canvas (10 holes per inch) comes only in standard-size sheets, which vary slightly depending on brand. They are 10½" x 13½" (106 x 136 holes) or 11" x 14" (108 x 138 holes).

Newer canvas like 5-count (5 holes per inch) and 14-count (14 holes per inch) are also becoming popular with plastic canvas designers.

Some canvas is soft and pliable, while other canvas is stiffer and more rigid. To prevent canvas from cracking during or after stitching, you'll want to choose pliable canvas for projects that require shaping, like round baskets with curved handles. If your project is a box or an item that will stand alone, stiffer canvas is more suitable.

Both 7- and 10-count canvas are available in a rainbow of colors. Most designs can be stitched on colored as well as clear canvas. When a pattern does not specify color in the materials list, you can assume clear canvas was used in the photographed model. If you'd like to stitch only a portion of the design, leaving a portion unstitched, use colored canvas to coordinate with yarn colors.

Buy the same brand of canvas for each entire project. Different brands of canvas may differ slightly in the distance between each bar.

Yarn & Other Stitching Materials

You may choose two-ply nylon plastic canvas yarn (the color numbers of two popular brands are found in Color Keys) or four-ply worsted-weight yarn for stitching on 7-count canvas. There are about 42 yards per ounce of plastic canvas yarn and 50 yards per ounce of worsted-weight yarn.

Worsted-weight yarn is widely available and comes in wool, acrylic, cotton and blends. If you decide to use worsted-weight yarn, choose 100% acrylic for best coverage. Select worsted-weight yarn by color instead of the color names or numbers found in the Color Keys. Projects stitched with worsted-weight yarn often "fuzz" after use. "Fuzz" can be removed by shaving with a fabric shaver to make your project look new again.

Plastic canvas yarn comes in over 60 colors and is a favorite of many plastic canvas designers. These yarns "wear" well both while stitching and in the finished product. When buying plastic canvas yarn, shop using the color names or numbers found in the Color Keys, or select colors of your choice.

Cutting Tools

You may find it helpful to have several tools on hand for cutting canvas. When cutting long, straight sections, scissors, craft cutters or kitchen shears are the fastest and easiest to use. For cutting out detailed areas and trimming nubs, you may like using manicure scissors, nail clippers or the Ultimate Plastic Canvas Cutters, available only from *The Needlecraft Shop* catalog (see address on page 160). If you prefer laying your canvas flat when cutting, try a craft knife and cutting surface — self-healing mats designed for sewing, as well as kitchen cutting boards, work well.

Needles & Other Stitching Tools

Blunt-end tapestry needles are used for stitching plastic canvas. Choose a No. 16 needle for stitching 5- and 7-count, a No. 18 for stitching 10-count, and a No. 24 for stitching 14- count. Keep a small pair of embroidery scissors handy for snipping yarn. Try using needle-nose jewelry pliers for pulling the needle through several thicknesses and out of tight spots.

Marking & Cutting Canvas

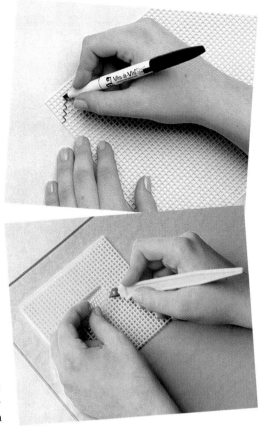

To avoid wasting canvas, careful cutting of each piece is important. For some pieces with square corners, you might be comfortable cutting the canvas without marking it beforehand. But for pieces with lots of angles and cutouts, you may want to mark your canvas before cutting.

To count holes on the graphs, look for the bolder lines showing each ten holes. These ten-count lines begin in the lower left-hand corner of each graph and are on the graph to make counting easier. To count holes on the canvas, you may use your tapestry needle, a toothpick or a plastic hair roller pick. Insert the needle or pick slightly in each hole as you count.

Most stitchers have tried a variety of marking tools and have settled on a favorite, which may be crayon, permanent marker or grease pencil. One of the best marking tools is a fine-point overhead projection marker, available at office supply stores. The ink is dark and easy to see and washes off complete-ly with water. After cutting and before stitching, it's important to remove all marks so they won't stain yarn as you stitch or show through stitches later. Cloth and paper toweling remove grease pencil and crayon marks, as do used fabric softener sheets.

Cutting Canvas

Follow all Cutting Instructions, Notes and labels above graphs to cut canvas. Each piece is labeled with a letter of the alphabet. Square-sided pieces are cut according to hole count, and some may not have graphs.

Unlike sewing patterns, graphs are not designed to be used as actual patterns but rather as counting, cutting and stitching guides. Therefore, graphs may not be actual size. Count the holes on the graph (see Marking & Cutting Canvas on page 151), mark your canvas to match, then cut. Trim off the nubs close to the bar, and trim all corners diagonally.

If you accidentally cut or tear a bar or two on your canvas, don't worry! Boo-boos can usually be repaired in one of several ways: heat the tip of a metal skewer and melt the canvas back together; glue torn bars with a tiny drop of craft glue, Super Glue® or hot glue; or reinforce the torn section with a separate piece of canvas placed at the back of your work. When reinforcing with extra canvas, stitch through both thicknesses.

Stitching the Canvas

Stitching Instructions for each section are found after the Cutting Instructions. First, refer to the illustrations of basic stitches on page 153 to familiarize yourself with the stitches used. Illustrations will be found near the graphs for pieces worked using special stitches. Follow the numbers on the tiny graph beside the illustration to make each stitch — bring your needle up from the back of the work on odd numbers and down through the front of the work on the even numbers.

Before beginning, read the Stitching Instructions to get an overview of what you'll be doing. You'll find that some pieces are stitched using colors and stitches indicated on graphs, and for other pieces you will be told which color and stitch to use to cover the entire piece.

Cut yarn lengths no longer than 18" to prevent fraying. Thread needle; do not tie a knot in the end. Bring your needle up through the canvas from the back, leaving a short length of yarn on the wrong side of the canvas. As you begin to stitch, work over this short length of yarn. If you are beginning with Continental Stitches, leave a 1" length,

but if you are working longer stitches, leave a longer length.

In order for graph colors to contrast well, graph colors may not match yarn colors. For instance, a light yellow may have been selected to represent the metallic cord color gold, or a light blue may represent white yarn.

When following a graph showing several colors, you may want to work all the stitches of one color at the same time. Some stitchers prefer to work with several colors at once by threading each on a separate needle and letting the yarn not being used hang on the wrong side of the work. Either way, remember that strands of yarn run across the wrong side of the work may show through the stitches from the front.

As you stitch, try to maintain an even tension on the yarn. Loose stitches will look uneven, and tight stitches will let the canvas show through. If your yarn twists as you work, you may want to let your needle and yarn hang and untwist occasionally.

When you end a section of stitching or finish a thread, weave the yarn through the back side of your last few stitches, then trim it off.

Construction & Assembly

After all pieces of an item needing assembly are stitched, you will find the order of assembly is listed in the Stitching Instructions and sometimes illustrated in diagrams found with the graphs. For best results, join pieces in the order written. Refer to the Stitch Key and to the directives near the graphs for precise attachments.

Finishing Tips

To combat glue strings when using a hot glue gun, practice a swirling motion as you work. After placing the drop of glue on your work, lift the gun slightly and swirl to break the stream of glue, as if you were making an ice cream cone. Have a cup of water handy when gluing. For those times when you'll need to touch the glue, first dip your finger into the water just enough to dampen it. This will minimize the glue sticking to your finger, and it will cool and set the glue more quickly.

To attach beads, use a bit more glue to form a cup around the bead. If too much shows after drying, use a craft knife to trim off excess glue.

Scotchguard® or other fabric protectors may be used on your finished projects. However, avoid using a permanent marker if you plan to use a fabric protector, and be sure to remove all other markings before stitching. Fabric protectors can cause markings to bleed, staining yarn.

For More Information

Sometimes even the most experienced needlecrafters can find themselves having trouble following instructions. If you have difficulty completing your project, write to:

Christmas Wonderland Editors,
The Needlecraft Shop,
23 Old Pecan Road, Big Sandy, Texas 75755.

BACKSTITCH

is usually used as an embroidery stitch to outline or add detail. Stitches can be any length and go in any direction.

BEAD ATTACHMENT ILLUSTRATION

CONTINENTAL STITCH

can be used to stitch designs or fill in background areas.

CROSS STITCH

can be used as a needle-point stitch or as an embroidery stitch, stitched over background stitches with contrasting yarn or floss.

FRENCH KNOT

is usually used as an embroidery stitch to add detail. Can be made in one hole or over a bar. If dot on graph is in hole, come up and go down with needle in same hole. If dot is across a bar or over grid, come up in one hole and go down one hole over.

LAZY DAISY STITCH

is usually used as an embroidery stitch to add detail. Can be any length and go in any direction. Come up and go down in same hole, leaving loop. Come up in another hole for top of stitch, put needle through loop and go down in same hole.

LONG STITCH

is a horizontal or vertical stitch used to stitch designs or fill in background areas. Can be stitched over two or more bars.

OVERCAST

is used to finish edges. Stitch two or three times in corners for complete coverage.

SLANTED GOBELIN STITCH

can be used to stitch designs or fill in background areas. Can be stitched over two or more bars in vertical or horizontal rows.

SMYRNA CROSS STITCH

can be used as a needlepoint stitch or as an embroidery stitch, stitched over background stitches with contrasting yarn or floss.

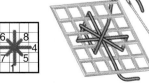

STRAIGHT STITCH

is usually used as an embroidery stitch to add detail. Stitches can be any length and can go in any direction. Looks like Backstitch except stitches do not touch.

WHIPSTITCH

is used to join two or more pieces together.

153

Fabrics

All counted cross stitch is worked on evenweave fabric, which means the horizontal and vertical threads are of the same thickness and are equally spaced. Evenweave fabric allows the cross stitches to form neat, even squares. There are many different styles, colors and thread counts available in evenweave fabrics.

The most popular fabric for counted cross stitch is Aida cloth. Aida is manufactured specifically for cross stitch and is available in a wide variety of colors and thread counts from 6 to 18. Most beginning cross-stitchers find Aida especially easy to work with because the holes for stitching are clearly visible.

Linen is made from fibers of the flax plant and is strong and durable. Its lasting quality makes it the perfect choice for heirloom projects. Linen is available in a range of muted colors and thread counts from 18 to 50. The weave of linen is finer than the weave of Aida cloth, and each cross stitch is worked over two threads.

Perforated paper and plastic are also used for cross stitching.

Needles

A cross stitch needle should be blunt, with a long, narrow eye. It should slip easily between the threads of the fabric, but should not pierce the fabric. For most cross stitch on fabric, size 24 or 26 tapestry needles work well. Some stitchers prefer to use a slightly smaller needle for backstitching.

The needle should glide through quickly and easily, requiring almost no effort from the stitcher. If your finger is getting sore from pushing the needle, or if you don't like to stitch without a thimble, your needle may be too big.

Hoops, Frames & Scissors

Hoops can be round or oval and come in many sizes. The three main types are plastic, spring-tension and wooden. Frames are easier on the fabric than hoops and come in many sizes and shapes. Once fabric is mounted it doesn't have to be removed until stitching is complete, saving fabric from excessive handling.

Small, sharp scissors are essential for cutting floss and removing mistakes. For cutting fabrics, invest in a top-quality pair of medium-sized sewing scissors. To keep them in top form, use these scissors only for cutting fabrics and floss.

CROSS STITCH (x):

There are two ways of making a basic Cross Stitch. The first method is used when working rows of stitches in the same color. The first step makes the bottom half of the stitches across the row, and the second step makes the top half.

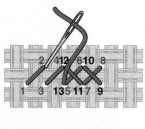

The second method is used when making single stitches. The bottom and top halves of each stitch are worked before starting the next stitch.

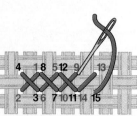

QUARTER CROSS STITCH (¼x):

Stitch may slant in any direction, as shown on graph.

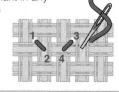

THREE-QUARTER CROSS STITCH (¾x):

A Half Cross Stitch plus a Quarter Cross Stitch. Stitch may slant in any direction, as shown on graph.

Preparing Fabric

Before you stitch, decide how large to cut fabric. If you are making a pillow or other design which requires a large unstitched area, be sure to leave plenty of fabric. If you are making a small project, leave at least 3" around all edges of design. Determine the design area size by using this formula: number of stitches across design area divided by the number of threads per inch of fabric equals size of fabric in inches. Measure fabric, then cut evenly along horizontal and vertical threads.

Reading Graphs

Cross stitch graphs may be black and white with symbols only, color only, or a combination of color and symbols. Each square on the graph represents one cross stitch over one square on Aida cloth or two or more threads on evenweave. Each graph has a color key, indicating floss numbers, colors and what type of stitch corresponds with each color or symbol.

Whenever used, abbreviations for items such as blending filament (BF) and pearl cotton (PC) will also be included.

Color keys have abbreviated headings for cross stitch (x), quarter cross stitch (¼x), three-quarter cross stitch (¾x) and backstitch (B'st). Some graphs are so large they must be divided for printing (see box at right).

Preparing Floss

The six strands of floss are easily separated, and the number of strands

Press out folds. To prevent raveling, hand overcast or machine zigzag fabric edges. Find center of fabric by folding horizontally and vertically, and mark with a small stitch.

used is given in instructions. Cut strands in 14"-18" lengths. When separating floss, always separate all six strands, then recombine the number of strands needed. To make floss separating easier, run cut length across a damp sponge. To prevent floss from tangling, run cut length through a fabric-softener dryer sheet before separating and threading needle. To colorfast red floss tones, which sometimes bleed, hold floss under running water until water runs clear. Allow to air dry.

WORKING FROM GRAPHS

Graphs or charts are made up of colors and symbols to tell you the exact color, type and placement of each stitch. Each square represents the area for one complete Cross Stitch. Next to each graph, there is a key with information about stitches and floss colors represented by the graph's colors and symbols.

Some graphs may be too large to fit on one page. When this happens, you'll find shaded areas given on the edge of one portion of the graph, indicating the area to be "overlapped" to complete the pattern. Stitch the shaded area only once.

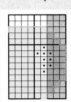

Stitch shaded area only once.

EMBROIDERY STITCHES
add detail and dimension to stitching. Unless otherwise noted, work Backstitches first, then other embroidery stitches.

BACKSTITCH
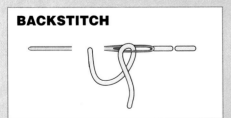

OUTLINE OR STEM STITCH

CHAIN STITCH
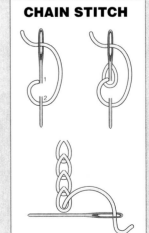

SATIN STITCH
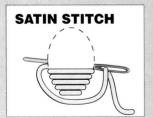

LAZY DAISY STITCH

FRENCH KNOT

Gauge

Always check your gauge before beginning a project. The purpose of checking gauge is to determine which hook size to use. The tightness or looseness of your stitches determines gauge, and is affected by hook size. Gauge is measured by counting the number of rows or stitches per inch.

Make a swatch at least 2" square in the stitch indicated in the gauge section of the pattern. Lay the swatch flat and measure the stitches and rows. If you determine you have more stitches or rows per inch than specified in the pattern, your gauge is too tight and you need to choose a larger hook. If you have fewer stitches or rows per inch than needed, a smaller hook is required.

For some patterns, especially small patterns like flowers or motifs, gauge is given as a size measurement for the entire motif. In this case, make one motif and measure.

Parentheses, Asterisks & More

For clarity, written instructions may include symbols such as parentheses, asterisks, brackets and diamonds. These symbols are used as signposts to set off a portion of instructions which will be worked more than once.

( ) Parentheses enclose instructions which are to be worked the number of times indicated after the parentheses. For example, "(2 dc in next st, skip next st) 5 times" means to follow the instructions within parentheses a total of five times. Parentheses may also be used to enclose a group of stitches which should be worked in one space or stitch. For example, "(2 dc, ch 2, 2 dc) in next st" means to work all the stitches within parentheses in the next stitch.

*Asterisks may be used alone or in pairs, many times in combination with parentheses. If used in pairs, a set of instruc-

tions enclosed within asterisks will be followed by instructions for repeating. These repeat instructions may appear later in the pattern or immediately after the last asterisk. For example, "*Dc in next 4 sts, (2 dc, ch 2, 2 dc) in corner sp*, dc in next 4 sts; repeat between ** 2 times" means to work through the instructions for repeating, then repeat only the instructions that are enclosed within the asterisks twice.

If used alone, an asterisk marks the beginning of instructions which are to be repeated. For example, "Ch 3, dc in same st, *ch 2, skip next 2 sts, dc in next st, ch 1, skip next st, 2 dc in next st; repeat from

* across" means to work from the beginning, then repeat only the instructions after the *, working all the way across the row. Instructions for repeating may also specify a number of times to repeat, and this may be followed by further instructions. For example, instructions might say, "...repeat from * 5 more times, dc in last st." To follow these instructions, work through from the beginning once, then repeat from * five more times for a total of six times. Then, follow remaining instructions, which in this example are "dc in last st."

[ ] Brackets and ◊ diamonds are also used to clarify and set off sec-

tions of instructions. In some patterns, all types of symbols are used together. As you can see, there is no need to be intimidated by symbols! These signposts will get you where you're going — to the end of a beautiful finished project.

ABBREVIATIONS

Chain(s)................................ch(s)	Single Crochet ....sc
Decrease.................................dec	Slip Stitch ....sl st
Double Crochet ....dc	Space(s) ....sp(s)
Half Double Crochet..............hdc	Stitch(es) ....st(s)
Increase ....inc	Together ....tog
Loop(s)................................lp(s)	Treble Crochet..........................tr
Round(s)............................rnd(s)	Yarn Over ....yo

CHAIN (ch)
Yo, draw hook through lp.

SLIP STITCH (sl st)
Insert hook in st, yo, draw through st and lp on hook.

FRONT LOOP / BACK LOOP (front lp/back lp)

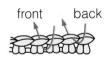

front   back

SINGLE CROCHET (sc)
Insert hook in st (A), yo, draw lp through, yo, draw through both lps on hook (B).

HALF DOUBLE CROCHET (hdc)
Yo, insert hook in st (A), yo, draw lp through (B), yo, draw through all 3 lps on hook (C).

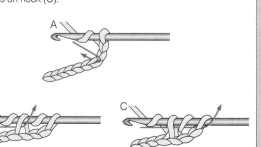

DOUBLE CROCHET (dc)
Yo, insert hook in st (A), yo, draw lp through (B), (yo, draw through 2 lps on hook) 2 times (C and D).

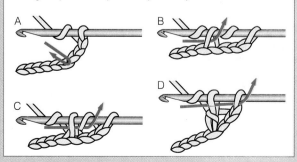

TREBLE CROCHET *(tr)*

Yo 2 times, insert hook in st (A), yo, draw lp through (B), (yo, draw through 2 lps on hook) 3 times (C, D and E).

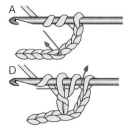

SINGLE CROCHET COLOR CHANGE *(sc color change)*

Drop first color; yo with 2nd color, draw through last 2 lps of st.

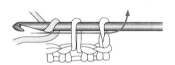

DOUBLE CROCHET COLOR CHANGE *(dc color change)*

Drop first color; yo with 2nd color, draw through last 2 lps of st.

SINGLE CROCHET next two stitches together *(sc next 2 sts tog)*

Draw up lp in each of next 2 sts, yo, draw through all 3 lps on hook.

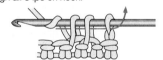

HALF DOUBLE CROCHET next two stitches together *(hdc next 2 sts tog)*

(Yo, insert hook in next st, yo, draw lp through) 2 times, yo, draw through all 5 lps on hook.

FRONT POST STITCH – fp:
BACK POST STITCH – bp:

Yo, insert hook from right to left around post of st on previous row, complete as dc.

front   back

REVERSE SINGLE CROCHET *(reverse sc)*

Working from left to right, insert hook in next st to the right (A), yo, draw through st, complete as sc (B).

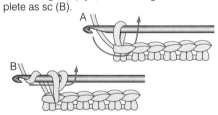

DOUBLE CROCHET next 2 stitches together *(dc next 2 sts tog)*

*Yo, insert hook in next st (A), yo, draw lp through (B), yo, draw through 2 lps on hook (C); repeat from * one time (D, E and F), yo, draw through all 3 lps on hook (G).

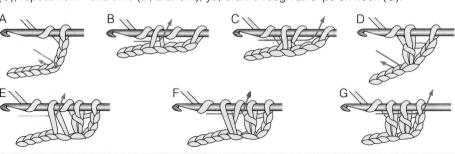

We would like to express our appreciation to the many people who helped create this book. Our special thanks go to each of the talented designers who contributed original designs.

Thanks, also, to all the talented and skilled editors, photographers and production staff whose technical expertise made this book come together.

In addition, we would like to thank the companies and individuals who provided locations for photography, models, props and other contributions.

Finally, we wish to express our gratitude to the following manufacturers for their generous contribution of materials and supplies and the stitchers who turn designers' dreams into works of art:

AD-TECH™
* *Crafty Magic Melt Princess glue gun* — Gingerbread Village, Bells & Bows

ALEENE'S™
* *Designer Tacky Glue* — Victorian Trinkets, Guardian Angels, Radiant Messenger, Ribbon Candy Bow, Baby's First Christmas, Night Jewels Ornaments, Sweets for the Chef

BAG WORKS
* *Apron* — Sweets for the Chef

BLACK & DECKER®
* *2 Temp™ glue gun* — Guardian Angels, Monogram Bookmarks

CADILLAC CO.
* *Craft globes* — Globe Game

CHARLES CRAFT, INC.
* *Aida* — Petite Samplers, Frosty & Family, Joyous Sentiments
* *Fiddlers Lite®* — Peaceful Hearts
* *Place mat and bread cover* — French Horn Trio
* *Collar* — Candy Cane Collar
* *Towel* — Joyous Sentiments

COATS & CLARK
* *Speed-Cro-Sheen®* — Crystal Snowflakes
* *Anchor embroidery floss* — Petite Samplers

DARICE®
* *Canvas* — Toy Soldier Quartet, Gingerbread Village, Tiny Additions, Keepsake Gift Tags, Radiant Messenger, Monogram Bookmarks, Celestial Beauty
* *Metallic & pearlized cords* — Victorian Trinkets, Celebrations Quilts, Celestial Beauty, Radiant Messenger, Celestial Accents, Baby's First Christmas, Night Jewels Ornaments
* *Nylon Plus™ yarn* — Victorian Trinkets, Celebration Quilts, Radiant Messenger, Ribbon Candy Bow

DMC CORPORATION
* *Pearl cotton* — Guardian Angels, Gingerbread Village, Toy Soldier Quartet, Monogram Bookmarks, Cat & Mouse, Globe Game, Tiny Additions
* *Embroidery floss* — Monogram Bookmarks, Keepsake Gift Tags, Welcome Accents, Frosty & Family, Candy Cane Collar, Snowflake Table Set, Skating Kitties, Joyous Sentiments, Peaceful Hearts
* *Cebelia (size 10)* — Golden Lace Globes, Blossoms in the Snow

FAIRFIELD PROCESSING CORP.
* *Poly-Fil Stuffing* — Guardian Angels

FREUDENBERG NONWOVENS
* *Pellon® Wonder Under®* — Sweets for the Chef, French Horn Trio
* *Stitch-n-Tear®* — Sweets for the Chef, French Horn Trio

JHB INT'L, INC.
* *Buttons* — Gingerbread Village

KREINIK
* *Metallic braid* — Toy Soldier Quartet, Monogram Bookmarks, Sacred Words, Miniature Beaded Ornaments
* *Blending filament* — Frosty & Family, Joyous Sentiments, Skating Kitties

MILL HILL/GAY BOWLES SALES, INC.
* *Seed beads* — Monogram Bookmarks, Miniature Beaded Ornaments

OFFRAY
* *Satin ribbon* — Guardian Angels

ONE AND ONLY CREATIONS®
* *Doll hair* — Guardian Angels, Celestial Beauty

RAINBOW GALLERY, INC.
* *Metallic yarn* — Guardian Angels

RHODE ISLAND TEXTILES CO.
* *RibbonFloss™* — Tiny Additions, Keepsake Gift Tags

SPINRITE®
* *Plastic canvas yarn* — Bells & Bows

UNIEK® CRAFTS
* *Metallic cord* — Toy Soldier Quartet
* *Needloft® yarn* — Guardian Angels, Celestial Beauty, Celestial Accents, Toy Soldier Quartet, Rosebuds & Ribbons, Cat & Mouse, Globe Game, Sweetheart Treasure Box

ZWEIGART®
* *Jubilee* — Welcome Accents
* *Valerie* — Snowfall Table Set
* *Afghan fabric* — Skating Kitties

SPECIAL CREDITS
* *Petite Samplers* — Project stitched by Diane Stitcher for Celia Lange Designs
* *Skating Kitties* — Project stitched by Janet Giese for Janelle Marie Designs

ACKNOWLEDGEMENTS

For supplies, first shop your local craft and needle-work stores. If you are unable to find the supplies you need, write to the address below for a free catalog. The Needlecraft Shop carries plastic canvas in a variety of shapes, sizes and colors, 60 colors of plastic canvas yarn and a large selection of pattern books.

**23 Old Pecan Road
Big Sandy, Texas 75755 (903) 636-4000**